FALSE
JUSTICE

FALSE JUSTICE

Unveiling the Truth About Social Justice

Stuart Greaves

© Copyright 2012–Stuart Greaves

All rights reserved. This book is protected by the copyright laws of the United States of America. This book may not be copied or reprinted for commercial gain or profit. The use of short quotations or occasional page copying for personal or group study is permitted and encouraged. Permission will be granted upon request. Unless otherwise identified, Scripture quotations are taken from the New King James Version. Copyright © 1982 by Thomas Nelson, Inc. Used by permission. All rights reserved.

DESTINY IMAGE₀ PUBLISHERS, INC.
P.O. Box 310, Shippensburg, PA 17257-0310
"Promoting Inspired Lives."

This book and all other Destiny Image, Revival Press, MercyPlace, Fresh Bread, Destiny Image Fiction, and Treasure House books are available at Christian bookstores and distributors worldwide.

For a U.S. bookstore nearest you, call 1-800-722-6774.
For more information on foreign distributors, call 717-532-3040.
Reach us on the Internet: www.destinyimage.com.

ISBN 13 TP: 978-0-7684-4196-3
ISBN 13 Ebook: 978-0-7684-8753-4

For Worldwide Distribution, Printed in the U.S.A.
1 2 3 4 5 6 7 8 / 16 15 14 13 12

Dedication

To my niece, Mahan Gabriella.

I know that You can do everything,
And that no purpose of Yours can be withheld from You
(Job 42:2).

To my nephew, Hasen Justice.

*The God of our fathers has chosen you that you should know His will, and see **the Just One**, and hear the voice of His mouth. For you will be His witness to all men of what you have seen and heard (Acts 22:14-15).*

Acknowledgments

Special thanks to Holly Fields, Stephanie Cantrell, Alisha Powell, Amanda Beattie, Alina Martiniuc , Bret Mavrich and Katie Bolling who all put countless hours helping make this book project a reality.

For God is not unjust to forget your work and labor of love which you have shown toward His name, in that you have ministered to the saints, and do minister (Hebrews 6:10).

Endorsements

This book contains a timely and foundational message to anyone who desires to touch the poor and oppressed of the earth. Solidly grounded in the truths of Scripture and filled with careful insights into the dangers of undertaking justice ministries without a right paradigm of Jesus, *False Justice* gives the theological underpinnings for cultivating a Christ-centered outworking of justice.

ALLEN HOOD
President of the International
House of Prayer University

This emerging generation has been apprehended by a burning call to bring forth Justice in the earth. But Justice without Jesus can be a global exercise in humanistic paradise building. My friend Stuart Greaves, writing with a profound prophetic wisdom from heaven, will help this passionate generation bring forth true justice that will flow down like a mighty river and preserve it from the muddy waters of a humanistic justice alliance that ultimately leads to a worship of man himself. Let Jesus, the champion of Justice, be exalted.

LOU ENGLE
President of TheCall, Inc.

False Justice gives a biblical perspective on the issue of justice that will help us to do works of compassion within the context of truth. Critical for the next generation of intercessory abolitionists who want to tear down slavery, trafficking, and all forms of injustice, it provides clear warnings of errors that must be avoided and the truths in the heart of God that must become the framework for all the contending we do over issues of injustice in the place of prayer.

BENJAMIN NOLOT
President and Founder of Exodus Cry

Stuart Greaves is a man who seeks to live a life of knowing Jesus, and making Him known. He carries one of the clearest and strongest prophetic teaching anointing that I've ever witnessed. His book, *False Justice*, emerges not from someone who is studying trends from a distance, but from an intercessor who carries a heart for true biblical justice: The Gospel. The subject of justice is the "hot topic" both in the church and in the world today, and there are many opinions and ideas in both places that are more opposed to the purposes of God than we realize. In this book, Stuart awakens us to the false justice movement, and then takes us through the Word to show us true justice.

COREY RUSSELL
Director of the Forerunner Program
at the International House of Prayer University

Stuart Greaves wisely and expertly tackles the subject of social justice with truth and scriptural light. *False Justice* reminds us not to lose our way in our concern for the poor and hurting, but to see Jesus as the Christ through whom all justice will come. Through prayer, fasting, and worship we are His partners on the earth for true spiritual and social justice. This book is a must read. Give it to your friends. Pray, seek the Lord. Contend for justice.

RACHEL HAUCK
Award-winning, best-selling author

"If we are to identify "true justice" we must discern and understand "false justice". Stuart's book is a must for anyone who wants to successfully navigate the deceptive fog of this age. As Stuart brilliantly explains, a colossal injustice is taking place among the nations—it is worse than hunger, genocide, human trafficking, and abortion—it is the lack of instruction and revelation on the knowledge of God. Stuart Greaves is a profound thinker, an anointed theologian and a man of prayer…you rarely find that combination of skills in one man…I highly recommend you read this book several times!"

PABLO PEREZ
Director of the Forerunner Music Academy

Most of the world is at war in some expression today and humanity is hopelessly divided on the nature, causes and cures of this time of social turbulence. Our whole media system seems to be a part of the reason for the increased violence. Almost to the last person on earth, if we were questioned as to whether we stood for justice in the world, would answer with an unhesitating YES! But our global attempts at stopping injustice and establishing justice appear to be sources of further division. Stuart Greaves has sounded a relevant principle in the war between opposing ideas of what justice appears to be. It seems to be summed up in: NO CHRIST, NO JUSTICE; KNOW CHRIST, KNOW JUSTICE. He affirms that every attempt and movement toward justice that is not Christocentric will not only end in failure but will introduce conditions characterized by less justice than before. Jesus is our great hope for true justice. This is a splendid book, well-written and balanced with clear directions and wise principles as a working grid for true justice.

JACK TAYLOR
President, Dimensions Ministries

Most of the musicians I meet today have an outcry against the injustices of the world but they often do not know what to do with this cry. As a worshipper, I see the gap between what is and what should be and it causes me to long for the wrong things to be made right. I think this book will give musicians, singers, worship leaders and songwriters some of the clarity they need to proclaim the message of Jesus, the King who loves justice even more than we do.

MISTY EDWARDS
Worship Leader and Sr. Leader at IHOP-KC

Contents

Foreword

One indicator signaling the return of Jesus is the widespread proliferation of demonic doctrines to deceive the Church. False teachers will lure the body of Christ away with teachings that seem harmless, but that are disastrous because they undermine the truth about Jesus and our loyalty to Him. What makes deceptive teachings and philosophies so dangerous is that they contain a measure of truth. Errant teachings contain biblical themes such as love, mercy, and justice.

The subject of justice is a common topic today—being discussed by preachers, singers, writers, and bloggers. Injustice and suffering have a special way of stirring our passion, and they should do so. The plight of the poor burdens us and even makes us angry. And the Bible has much to say on these topics. The Church must be deeply involved in justice; Jesus is the king of justice.

But there is a greater injustice in the earth occurring right now, bigger than hunger, genocide, human trafficking, abortion, or any of the other massive problems we grieve over and long to address. The greatest injustice is the lack of teaching on the majesty of Christ Jesus and the knowledge of God. Yet so often, the discussion of justice is centered on something else—imagining that so long as we are focused on the poor or on solving justice issues, we are in the way of Jesus and in keeping with Christianity. This is an error.

As Stuart so clearly conveys, there is a false justice movement that is actually in opposition to Christ and His kingdom. Like a Trojan horse, some blindly receive any and all input regarding justice, completely unaware that many are trying to establish justice that is disconnected from the truth of Jesus. Meanwhile, the false justice movement has its prophets, songwriters, and even a message that undermines the apostolic gospel and ends in perdition.

Any teaching on justice that compromises or undermines Jesus' divinity, humanity, death, resurrection, ascension, or return has the potential to lead people into a vision for renewal that is in direct competition with Christ and His kingdom.

While it is true that the danger to be led away from the truth of the gospel is grave, I believe God is raising up messengers who will call the church back to her first love. These messengers will lead the body Christ into giving extravagantly to the poor, but out of a place of deep affection for Jesus—His person, His work, and His ways.

Christ Jesus, in person and not just His principles, is the only lasting solution to injustice. His sacrifice for sin on the cross triumphed over injustice, and when He comes again He will set up His kingdom on the earth and "decide with equity for the poor."

In the meantime, He sits at His Father's right hand, with a promise that He will pour out His Spirit on His Church so we might experience revival and have power to significantly confront every injustice—from government corruption to cancer.

Stuart Greaves has been part of the International House of Prayer since its beginning in 1999. He is on our senior leadership team and is one of the main teachers in our Bible school, IHOPU. Stuart is a brilliant teacher of the Word, being a man of prayer who is deeply committed to sound, biblical teaching, and desires to see the people of God give themselves to one true passion: Jesus.

Stuart has been a gift to the IHOP Missions Base in the clarity of the message that God has given him. In my opinion, the message of *False Justice* is a very timely prophetic exhortation for the body of Christ. I believe it will enlarge your understanding of the Word, inspire your heart and challenge you to action just as it has done to the staff at the International House of Prayer. I recommend this book to all who love Jesus and want to do works of justice on God's terms.

MIKE BICKLE
Founder, International House of Prayer
Kansas City, Missouri

Part I

FALSE
JUSTICE

Chapter 1

Introduction

From a very young age, I was familiar with the plight of the poor. I grew up in a country called Suriname, a small nation on the northeast coast of South America. Both of my parents grew up very poor, and have always been very openhearted to the needy and willing to serve the less fortunate. Our family interacted with many different circles of people, from many different social classes and backgrounds.

In second grade, I began watching world news, which had a profound impact on me. I became aware of the world around me and of the different kinds of social justice dynamics at work on an international scale. My father was involved in Foreign Affairs, and when I was eleven years old he became a diplomat for Suriname in Caracas, Venezuela, which had significant poverty at that time. I again found myself surrounded by people of all social classes. At times I felt at home among the poorest of the poor who lived in the barrios, where the police do not usually venture because of the crowded, maze-like streets where one can easily get lost. I was not put off by these neighborhoods. I was disturbed by the inequality.

When I became a Christian at fourteen, I found there was a definite disconnect between my personal faith and the affinity I had towards the poor. I was a new believer with a compartmental-ized understanding of Jesus. I did not know how to combine my devotional life with my social concern.

I understood Jesus had compassion for the poor and wanted to feed them. But I did not understand His thoughts about the broader implications of social justice, like poor people getting pushed out of their neighborhoods by wealthy people moving in or socioeconomic disparity across racial lines.

As I grew in my faith, I learned about sanctification, heaven, the Lord's return, personal holiness, and sharing Christ with the lost. I believed in a personal Jesus who had a lot to say about my personal spirituality, but not much to say about social justice.

The Connection Between Christianity and Social Justice

It wasn't until a few years later, when I attended Southeastern University, a private Bible college in Lakeland, Florida, that I was confronted with the issue of how Christianity connects to social justice. On my campus, I ran into a group of students who had been deeply affected by liberal theology, challenging the theologi-cal views we were learning in the classroom. They were zealous about the subject of societal injustice and had a strong commit-ment to their views, desiring to effect change.

Due to my natural pull towards the issue of the poor and jus-tice, I often found myself in conversation with these students; but I did not agree with what they were saying. Their claims and beliefs dismissed and undermined clear, orthodox, evangelical theology; calling into question the nature of Christ, His mediation, His res-urrection, and His deity. I knew I could not agree with them on these points.

I was sure that what I had learned about Jesus up until that point was true; however, through my many discussions with these students, the Bible verses they highlighted brought to light the fact that my understanding was compartmentalized.

Their rhetoric did not win me over to their views but the Bible verses they quoted alerted me. These students discussed the Old Testament prophets and what they had said. I had not spent a lot of time in the Old Testament before then, but I was introduced to passages like Jeremiah 22:16 where the connection is made that hearing the cause of the poor and the needy is part of knowing God:

> *He judged the cause of the poor and needy; then it was well. Was not this knowing Me?" says the Lord* (Jer. 22:16).

I had always understood my walk of knowing Jesus in the context of my quiet time, character development, and sharing my faith when I had occasion to; but the idea that intimacy with God extended into "judging the cause of the poor and needy" was entirely foreign to me.

My interaction with these fellow students began to confront some of my preconceived ideas. For instance, when reading the story of Sodom and Gomorrah (see Gen. 19:1-29), the personal way in which I saw the Bible influenced my premise that Sodom and Gomorrah were judged for their immorality. I failed to recognize that, according to Ezekiel, they were destroyed based on the social indictments against them:

> *Look, this was the iniquity of your sister Sodom: She and her daughter had pride, fullness of food, and abundance of idleness; neither did she strengthen the hand of the poor and needy. And they were haughty and committed abomination before Me; therefore I took them away as I saw fit* (Ezek. 16:49-50).

Though immorality was practiced in the culture of Sodom and undoubtedly was part of the reason for God's judgment, this was never the stated purpose in scripture for their destruction. The reason for Sodom's judgment was more incriminating and applicable to many of us. God judged Sodom because of pride, overeating, excessive time wasting, and overlooking the poor.

God's Plan for Redemption

In the prophets, I discovered a God who, through the Cross of Christ, is executing His plan of redemption for entire people groups, nations, and even the planet. Isaiah, Ezekiel, Amos, Hosea, Jeremiah, and the other prophetic voices of the Old Testament seemed to have something to say about a God who is deeply committed to seeing justice brought forth on the earth.

I began to make sense of this Jesus who came to take away the sins of the world both individually and socially. I began to understand the One who would both renew a believer's soul and renew the societies of the earth. I never entered into a crisis of faith as I discovered these facets of Jesus, but I was being thrust into another arena of thinking.

When I was a college senior, I began seeking the Lord about the subject of justice. Because of the poverty I witnessed growing up, I often wondered if God was calling me to work among the poor. He began to speak to me through the scriptures about poverty, oppression, government, and justice.

My vision and faith were beginning to expand and I was seeing Jesus, the God of justice, throughout the Word. Around this time a colleague of mine introduced me to the life of St. Francis of Assisi. I had never seriously looked at St. Francis' life, and as I began to read I was deeply moved by his commitment to prayer, fasting, holiness, preaching, and touching the poor.

On various occasions I would make real concerted efforts to move to the inner city, but the Lord would surprisingly always close the doors. After several years, the Lord directed my wife, Esther, and me to move to Kansas City to be a part of the International House of Prayer of Kansas City, a ministry that is focused on 24/7 prayer for justice and doing 24/7 works of justice.

Then, about five years into my time with IHOP-KC, while I was giving leadership to the NightWatch (midnight-6 a.m.), I hit an existential crisis and began to wrestle intensely over the direction and purpose of my life.

It was a season of great tension for me. I had a deep desire for impact and was wondering whether or not I had made the best decision to be involved in the prayer movement. I questioned whether I was using the full potential of my gifts and talents. I could not see the fuller connection between the worship movement and touching the poor.

I began seeking the Lord and wondering if it was time for Esther and me to go live among the poor. I was grappling with other questions as well: If we moved what would we do? What would it be like? What would our objectives be?

In my college years, I had wanted to travel around the world and go to the poorest places of the earth. I was asking the Lord if the time to make that trip was now. Two of my friends had just returned from Italy and told me about their visit with Franciscan monks. I began thinking about going to Assisi, Italy to visit St. Francis' monastery.

One morning, a few weeks into this crisis, I woke up out of a dead sleep and heard the Holy Spirit say, "Go to Mexico City." This direction from the Lord made no sense to me. I had no contacts in Mexico City and no idea what I would do there. I went on with my day, pondering why the Lord would direct me to Mexico City.

I had been thinking about a dear friend of mine who lived in Florida, with whom I had often discussed issues concerning the poor and justice. I really wanted to see him. I had not talked with him for some time about these things, and thought it would be good to reconnect and get some counsel from him.

When I called him to see if we could meet he said, "I would love to meet with you. You can meet me in Florida in three weeks or you can meet me in Mexico City next week. I am going there with a group of college students." I could not believe my ears.

I joined my friend and the group of young adults in Mexico City. We had hours of discussions about justice. We spent time among the poor, and afterwards we would debrief and study the Word. When it was time to sleep, I paired up six hard chairs against each other to make a bed. This was a perfect situation for me: I was among the poor; I had a luxurious bed; and I was able to spend a lot of time in small group study and alone with the Lord concerning the issue of justice.

One morning the students invited me to go on a road trip with them. I am not much of a sightseer, but I agreed to join them. I had no idea where we were going, but as we were nearing our destination about two hours outside of Mexico City, I realized we were on our way to a monastery.

The tour guide explained that Dominicans now ran the monastery, but it had originally been used by Franciscans. When he said that, I realized the Lord was ambushing me. I began to feel His tangible presence resting on me, and I separated myself from the group to be alone and think and pray about the issue of the poor and justice.

I began to feel disturbed in my spirit about the issue of theological compromise related to the subject of social justice. I went from wrestling about my own purpose in life to wrestling theologically. I began to realize that there is a justice that God desires and one that is humanistic.

The Only True Theology for Social Justice

When we returned to the place we were staying, I still had a sense of the presence of the Lord on my heart. Suddenly the Holy Spirit spoke to me: *"The present social justice movement is preparing the poor of the earth to receive the Antichrist."*

His words shook me at the core of my being. I did not expect Him to say what He said and did not even see the truth of what He spoke until I heard it from heaven. From that moment, I began to see scripture through a different lens. It was the first time things truly began to integrate for me. I began to see the gospel truly as the answer for every sphere of society instead of vacillating between the personal gospel and the social gospel.

The personal gospel often does not translate into social concern, and social concern may not translate into personal holiness. This compartmentalization of Jesus and His gospel has left a theological vacuum, leaving many to have their questions answered by searching out other ideologies and false messengers instead of searching out the heart of God through Christ and His word.

Jesus has made all the necessary provision for justice on the earth through His death, burial, resurrection, and unfolding His Father's eternal plan for justice. This plan is being manifest now in part, but will be fully made evident when Jesus returns. He alone will accomplish justice among the nations—not another god or any pantheon of gods.

Some are suggesting that all the faiths of the world should join together. Beloved, Jesus is not in a discussion with Muhammad and Buddha about justice. Jesus is not at the council table with the very forces of darkness that He came to destroy (see 1 John 3:8). Christ alone has the answer—as found in His gospel—for true justice in the world.

The experience in Mexico set me on a journey to find out: What does Jesus have to say about justice? What is His plan for justice now and in the coming age? How will He go about accomplishing justice?

One of my favorite passages on this in the Old Testament is found in Isaiah 42, where the prophet declares God's strategy for justice and that it is a plan clearly established before the foundation of the earth. Justice is in the heart of the Lord Jesus Christ and He alone will establish it in every sphere of society in the world. The gospel of Jesus Christ is the only true theology of social justice and hope for the poor.

Chapter 2

The Progression of Justice

"Lord, why not abort the child?" I prayed, as for about thirty seconds abortion seemed reasonable to me.

In 1997, after finals week and graduation from college, my father requested to meet me in the pastor's office. I had no way of knowing what I was about to find out. My father began to share how he felt about my sister, Nayomi, and me, and suddenly he began to cry. I remember it so vividly.

My father proceeded to tell me that my sister, who was a junior in college, had gotten pregnant. I was devastated and very concerned about how she and her unborn child would be provided for. My sister was an international student at that time and, therefore, unable to work. Being in a similar situation, I did not have many resources, either. I began to realize that some of the provision for this child would fall upon my parents.

Throughout that whole week I was burdened about my sister's life and future. One afternoon in my room, on my knees before the Lord, praying for my beloved sister and feeling the challenges of the situation, suddenly, aborting the baby seemed like a reasonable alternative. Something so dark, evil, and sinister actually made real sense to me for about thirty seconds—right in the middle of seeking the Lord.

It was one of the most surreal experiences of my life. After a few moments, I realized the utter selfishness of my soul, and repented before heaven for having even considered murder a viable option to a difficult situation.

At that time in my life, I had a very clear position on the issue of abortion. I was a member of a congregation where the leadership of the church had taken an active stance to defend the rights of the unborn and contend for a culture of life. I was deeply involved in my church: I was a part of the leadership team of a youth church, was part of the prophecy team, a bass player on the worship team, led a home group, traveled on mission trips, and tried to seek the Lord to the best of my ability. Not only that, for some time I had been pursuing the cultivation of a lifestyle of seeking the Lord for revival. I did not fit the "profile" of one who would even consider abortion an option, or so I thought.

I was horribly surprised to discover the depth of murder in my own heart. I realized at that moment that there was no difference between myself and those who have gone through with an abortion or those who administer it. Except for the grace of God, there go I.

I wanted justice for my sister, for the burden she would bear. I wanted to relieve myself of any responsibility, implied or real. So for a few moments, I meditated on man's brand of justice for unwanted pregnancy—abortion.

The Core Issue of Justice

The core issue of justice is to have right standing with the Godhead through Jesus Christ. Without Him, there is no justice. The day Adam broke fellowship with God is when injustice entered into the world,

For all have sinned and fall short of the glory of God,
being justified freely by His grace through the redemption
that is in Christ Jesus, whom God set forth as a propi-
tiation by His blood, through faith, to demonstrate His
righteousness, because in His forbearance God had passed
over the sins that were previously committed, to demon-
strate at the present time His righteousness, that He might
be just and the justifier of the one who has faith in Jesus
(Rom. 3:23-26).

In our pursuit of justice, this truth must be our starting point; otherwise, we will end up self-righteous. When the Bible talks about justice, it shows it as that which leads to *shalom*. Though *shalom* is most commonly recognized as meaning "peace", its meaning is more nuanced than that alone. The "peace" of *shalom* carries the connotation of completeness, prosperity, health, salvation, and wholeness.[1] This *shalom* is the end result of God's justice coming forth on the earth.

So justice, simply defined, is removing the wrongs that hinder right or removing the obstacles of *shalom*. Most people think of justice only as punitive, but justice is far more than that. God's justice is about wholeness and divine order of everything that He has created. We usually think of justice operating within the social and legal realm; however, God's justice encompasses every sphere, both spiritual and natural, including the environment, our homes, our workplaces, governments, friendships, and our inner life. At its core, justice is about everything being made whole.

For example, justice operates in the spirit realm when someone becomes a follower of Christ or when demonic activity in the human soul is put to an end. We see justice in our environment when nature functions the way God intended it to, with its resources stewarded well and cultivated into maximum fruitfulness. Justice includes physical healing, where wrong things are set right within the human body, such as the restoration of a withered hand (see Matt. 12:10) or the opening of blind eyes (see Matt. 9:27-30; 12:22; 21:14; Mark 10:51-52; John 9:6-7). Justice also involves ending societal problems such as abortion, human trafficking, poverty, racism, and other systemic injustices.

Justice, in essence, is when all things are reconciled to God (see 1 Cor. 15:24-27). Jesus brings the divine order between God and all that is in creation. From the very beginning, creation was founded on justice. When God called all that He had made "good," before sin had entered the world, creation was in right and divine order.

This vision for divine order sets the stage for how we must view justice today. Justice has a three-fold progression. First, it starts with God confronting the depravity of the human heart, whether we are the oppressor or the oppressed. Second, justice confronts the sin between people on both an individual and a societal level, including the unjust ways we ourselves treat others.

It is only after we have grasped the first two areas of justice that we can really evaluate the third, which is the injustice committed against us—both the oppression that we receive as individuals and that which we receive as part of a corporate social group.

To be clear, this is a *paradigmatic* progression, not necessarily a *pragmatic* one. In other words, it is not meant to dictate how we go about our deeds of justice; instead, it lays the foundation for how we understand and process justice.

Usually, when we think of injustice, we either begin with the injustices we have personally experienced committed against us, or perhaps the injustice we see around us committed against others by others. Yet neither of these approaches really addresses the root issue: if the people involved in seeking justice are not reconciled to God, justice can never be fully executed on their behalf.

Injustice Committed Against God

So when we think about injustice, before we can rightly address any other issue, we must start with our injustices committed against

God. The day that Adam rebelled against God and broke fellowship with Him is the day that injustice entered into the world (see Gen. 3). From then on, Paul tells us that all have sinned and fallen short of the glory of God (see Rom. 3:23). *All* have sinned: male, female, black, white, rich, poor, Republican, Democrat, citizen of America, or member of Al-Qaeda—everyone who has ever lived. *All* have fallen short of the glory of God.

This is why the issue of justice starts with our need for right standing with God through faith in Christ. Without this, there is no justice. The born-again experience gains us right standing with God. This is the beginning of *shalom*, of justice.

Paul uses legal language to explain our need for being made right with God, calling it our *justification* (see Rom. 3:23-27). The purpose of heaven's court is to execute righteousness and justice, and so the beginning point of justice is humanity's need to be justified in the court of heaven. God's justice requires restitution by those who are guilty before Him. God, in His infinite mercy through Christ, sought to pay that restitution on behalf of those who choose to follow Christ's leadership. Those who do not accept His terms will be left on their own to pay their debt to God. The problem is that their debt is infinite, and it will take eternity to pay it off in the Lake of Fire. Until this justification is established in the hearts of people, we will continue to see rampant injustice in the public sphere.

This is not to say that external laws are unnecessary—far from it. In fact, laws can be effective in checking the outward manifestation of sin and keeping order in a society. We want to pray for righteous laws and systems to be put in place in our government, and we want to pursue them through the political means made available to us. We want to enact social mandates that oppose evil and support positive values. But we must keep the perspective that, at the end of the day, even though these external works of justice may improve society outwardly, they are powerless to bring about the internal transformation of the darkened human soul (see Isa. 64:6). In other words, men and women still need to come to the saving knowledge of Jesus Christ.

All throughout history, there have been many individual movements and ideas that have established outward change, both individually and socially, without the power to produce inward transformation. Paul calls these empty philosophies vain deceit and self-imposed religion (see Col. 2:8). Even if they succeed in restraining unjust behaviors, as long as they do not seek right standing with God through faith in Christ, no justice has ultimately been done.

In light of this, when we approach the issue of justice, we must start with restoring the fellowship with God through Christ that humanity lost at the Fall—a restoration of fellowship only found through Christ. Everything else flows from that reality. Justice begins on the inside, established by grace through faith.

This inward transformation should then manifest outwardly in doing justice in our homes, friendships, workplaces, and society. Having said that, external works of justice do not in and of themselves produce justice, but can testify to the authenticity of our born-again experience. Romans and James together affirm this—faith without works is dead (see James 2:20-26), but works apart from faith are ultimately empty and futile (see Rom. 3-4).

Just as we must acknowledge our personal injustices against God, we must acknowledge our culture's societal injustice against Him. Our societies endorse all sorts of injustice, such as participating in racism by passively benefiting from an oppressive system without taking a stand against it. They condone or even support various levels of extortion, immorality, and covetousness. The entertainment industry—the movies we watch and the music we listen to—shows the immorality in our culture. Our covetousness is exposed in the language of our commercials and advertising. Extortion is seen in the commercialization of the gospel, when men and women treat their public ministry as a platform to gain wealth and fame (see 1 Tim. 6:5; Titus 1:11; 2 Pet. 2:3, 15; Jude 1:11). Even as much as these practices wound other people, much more so, they grieve the holy heart of God.

We have to keep this in mind when confronting the subject of justice. There is not one person in the earth, nor a governmental system or political party, neither culture nor gender that is righteous by virtue of their social status. Every form of government we have had in six thousand years of human history has proven to us that no governmental system has what it takes to bring about true justice to the earth. The reason for this is simple: unredeemed men are leading the vast majority of the earth. This is why Jesus teaches us through the Lord's Prayer to ask for God's government to be established on the earth (see Matt. 6).

David understood that the darkness of man's heart makes him unable to produce justice in the earth:

> *The fool has said in his heart, "There is no God." They are corrupt, they have done abominable works, there is none who does good. The Lord looks down from heaven upon the children of men, to see if there are any who understand, who seek God. They have all turned aside, they have together become corrupt; there is none who does good, no, not one* (Ps. 14:1-3).

There is not one person who is righteous or does good. No nation is in a moral position to rid the world of evil. Jeremiah states this clearly when he tells us that the Lord has a controversy with all the nations:

> *...The Lord will roar from on high, and utter His voice from His holy habitation; He will roar mightily against His fold. He will give a shout, as those who tread the grapes, against all the inhabitants of the earth. A noise will come to the ends of the earth—for the Lord has a*

controversy with the nations; He will plead His case with all flesh. He will give those who are wicked to the sword… (Jer. 25:30-31).

Isaiah confirms this, telling us that Jesus is searching the earth, and yet He cannot find justice, righteousness, or truth anywhere in it.

Then the Lord saw it, and it displeased Him that there was no justice. He saw that there was no man, And wondered that there was no intercessor; Therefore His own arm brought salvation for Him; And His own righteousness, it sustained Him (Isa. 59:15-16).

We try to crusade for any number of causes without addressing any of the internal issues that are fueling the injustices. We rail against corporate greed and government corruption, but think nothing of stealing office supplies. We raise endless awareness campaigns about sex trafficking, but we give ourselves to lustful thoughts. We hold racial reconciliation summits, and yet we are not able to overcome our petty grudges (see Gen. 6:5). The truth of it is that we love the very injustices we are trying to fight.

I found this out the hard way the day I was praying for my sister. I was shocked at the level of agreement in my heart with something that I knew to be wicked. How did I get here? I began to realize that we can address various social injustices without addressing the very spirit of those things in our own personal lives. Our compartmentalized gospel is forcing us into a false dilemma: as Christians we feel as though we must either focus on personal holiness or social activism, but not both.

Both individuals and society are in need of right standing with God through His Son Jesus Christ. Jeremiah describes the human heart as wicked and deceitful beyond measure (see Jer. 2 and 17). It is because of our fallen condition that we have sinned against others through neglect, pride, and ambition. We need the saving grace of Christ to rescue us from our own ways. Without Christ, we will only continue to perpetuate injustices against one another.

Injustice Committed Against One Another

History has borne this out to be true. Fallen humanity has produced countless injustices. We see it in the family sphere: domestic violence, adultery, divorce, and child abuse. In the realm of government, injustice and inequity comes through our unjust wars, unjust immigration laws, police brutality, exorbitant medical care, unfair labor wages, and unproductive educational systems. Our societies have endorsed human trafficking, child labor, abortion, prostitution, racism, and misogyny.

When we look around and see such pervasive injustices committed by others we ask questions like, *"How can husbands beat their wives?"* *"How can an uncle rape his nephew?"* *"How can any person traffic young girls for profit?"* When we see fellow humans treating others in such an unjust manner, we are appalled.

Even so, these questions expose our own hearts as disconnected from unrighteousness. When thinking of injustice, our tendency is to limit our perception of it to our favorite justice issues—often very large issues such as slavery, genocide, or similar atrocities. It is easy to disconnect ourselves from such a picture, yet injustice is much broader than those things. In so many ways we ourselves have committed injustices in our homes, in our churches, our work place, and our communities.

For example, we supplant our coworker because we are caught up in getting a promotion. We are driven by our competitive nature, our petty rivalries, and bitter jealousies. We envy the prosperity and success of our neighbors and friends instead of rejoicing with them (see Rom. 12:15). We fail to restrain our speech—lying, gossiping, and slandering one another. James goes so far as to say that our religion—which includes our works of justice—is worthless if we fail to curb our tongues (see James 1:26-27).

We get mad at the racism in society, but we avoid our brother in the church who has offended us. We cry out against the greed of global financiers, but we refuse to confront the covetousness of our own souls while building arguments against tithing, generosity, or lifestyles that enhance our ability to give to kingdom purposes. Some get angry with world leaders for not handling their national budget, but will not even balance their own checkbooks. Our national spending upsets us, but it is we who are the exorbitant consumers. In short, we cannot bind the injustice in society that also binds us.

But when we start with acknowledging our own injustice against God and are honest about the injustices we ourselves have committed against others, it will actually keep us from becoming self-righteous when we confront the injustices others commit. Understanding the progression of justice will produce humility and compassion within us so that we can maintain a humble spirit and a heart of gratitude, without wrongly evaluating others.

We are called to embrace the cross, acknowledging that we have sinned against both God and man, and receive the born-again experience. While there is a measure of restraint of wickedness that can be found through external law, that alone cannot bring about the lasting transformation that Christ desires in His new kingdom on earth.

Holiness Is Key in Our Efforts to Bring About Justice

True justice *always* originates in the heart of God and is brought forth as all things are reconciled to Him through Christ. In the present social justice movement there are believers who are truly justified before God, but are living in compromise, while still attempting to bring about justice on the earth. What ends up happening is that we become a people who attempt to do external works of justice, while neglecting the injustice in our own hearts. But if the foundation of the progression of justice is our right standing with God, then we must include holiness in our efforts.

Holiness is an inward disposition of our hearts, and justice is when that holiness is expressed through us into all the spheres of life and society. Jesus speaks of holiness in terms of washing a dish. He calls us to clean the inside of the cup *first*, that the outside might be clean also (see Matt. 23:23-28). He emphasizes the importance of the state of our hearts.

Too often, we think that the issue that lies before us is whether we should concern ourselves with the inside or the outside of the cup. Should we care more about being holy in our hearts or about going out to do good works? Such questions miss the point—Jesus calls us to focus on both. However, He says to clean the inside of the cup *first,* that the outside of the cup may be clean also.

The outside of the cup—the external issues of justice—cannot be changed permanently without changing the inside of the cup. This inward change comes through the biblical understanding of who Jesus is, as the Savior of our souls and the redeemer of society, and being in dynamic relationship with Him. We never have to choose between the gospel and social justice, because the gospel, as Jesus and His apostles preached it, is profoundly social in its implications. The gospel is the theology of justice. We will find ourselves as the light of the world and the salt of the earth—walking in personal holiness—which should, and will, translate to the way we impact society.

If we clean the inside of the cup in the way that Scripture calls us to be clean on the inside, confronting the issues of injustice in our heart like pride, envy and lust, it will affect the way we deal with societal issues of race, gender, abortion, human trafficking, child labor, prostitution, and misogyny. We cannot engage in pornography and, at the same time, fight against human trafficking. We cannot engage in bitterness, which Jesus calls murder (see Matt. 5:22), and take a stand against abortion. We cannot allow covetousness in our hearts to remain uncontested while taking a stand against poverty and economic disparity. We cannot bind in society what binds us.

Justice starts with our need to be justified by faith. Our faith is not just in the Jesus who saves our souls; our faith is in Christ the Messiah, the Savior of the societies of the earth. And this faith in Christ requires an active obeying of God, structuring our lives in the grace of God to walk in the way the Lord has designed for us.

Micah says that it is required of us to do works of justice, to love mercy, and to intimately and humbly walk with Jesus (see Mic. 6:8). This is how the just shall live. If we begin to live that way within the context of the privacy of our own hearts, then it will overflow into the other spheres of life that we are concerned about. True personal holiness will always lead to social justice.

Chapter 3

False Messengers

I believe that we are living in the beginning of the generation in which the Lord is going to return. The scripture makes it very clear that no one knows the day or the hour (see Matt. 24:36); however, we are commanded to know the signs of the times (see Mark 13:32). However, the Lord is not going to return at any moment.

According to the Scripture, there are still many things that need to take place for that day to come. However, it would not surprise me if there are people alive on the earth today who will witness the return of the Lord. The generation in which the Lord is going to return is the most described generation in the Word of God. There is more information about this generation than any other generation in redemptive history, including the generation of the Lord's First Coming. There are many passages in the word of God that address this.[2] One of these passages is Matthew 24.

In Matthew 24, the disciples came to Jesus privately, and began asking Him about the sign of His coming and of the end of the age. Jesus' answer needs to be noted—He does not give them an indifferent response. He starts out by giving them a strong warning concerning the issue of truth. There are two other passages in the gospels where this story is repeated, and Jesus starts out the same way (see Mark 13:5; Luke 21:8). He warns His disciples about the issue of truth. When addressing this issue in the second letter to the church of Thessalonica, Paul starts out with the same concern (see 2 Thess. 2:3, 7).

One of the things that Jesus addresses is that many will come and even say that Jesus is the Christ, yet they will be filled with many false ideas and concepts. This happens during a time when there are all kinds of troubles and injustices taking place in the earth.

Many will be asking questions about justice and peace as a result of this—seeking answers when it comes to the racial strife, unjust and corrupt wars between nations, and all manner of famines and diseases that will be on the earth (see Matt. 24:6-7). Jesus tells us that during that time many false messengers will arise, both false prophets and false christs.

False Prophets and False Christs

The deception that Jesus warns us about happens in two ways. First, it turns our eyes away from the truth of Jesus. Second, it makes humanity's principles of right and wrong the foundation of justice rather than the right standards of Jesus Christ. This deception will cause us to become wise in our own opinions. Jesus warns us that there will be false prophets and false christs. The scripture warns us that the enemy will raise up false messengers at the end of the age. The Bible refers to them as false prophets and false christs (see Matt. 24:24).

These false messengers will get our eyes off of the truth of Christ and bolster the nations in their self-reliance and false confidence in their ability to establish justice in the earth (see Isa. 64:7). Some of these messengers will be more covert in their deception, whereas others will be more overt in their deception. Regardless of how they present themselves, Jesus says that they are wolves in sheep's clothing (see Matt 7:15).

These messengers have a presentation that is appealing as they claim to bring justice and peace, yet their insights will cause many to fall prey to perdition. They get our eyes off of the personhood of Christ, denying the truth of His nature as fully God in His very essence from eternity past and fully man born by a virgin. Secondly, they bolster us in our own sense of just and moral standing before God by rejecting the atoning work of the death, burial, and resurrection of Jesus Christ.

The entry point of these false messengers is often the injustices of others committed against others, which, in the progression of justice, is the final place we want to end up as we think about justice. The emphasis is on the social sin at the expense of our personal sin, while failing to recognize that the fundamental cause of social sin is individual depravity. The scriptures make it very clear that personal depravity is the root cause of social sin.

By the time our communities or nations are facing social sin, personal depravity has already become full-blown. Social sin is the summation of expressed personal depravity. For instance, we can see an example of this in the murder of Able. Cain slaying his brother was the fruit of him refusing to deal with his internal anger and jealousy. These false messengers have ideologies that will either not address the inward life or have the power to transform the inward life. They are wolves in sheep's clothing. Outwardly, they have a manifestation of concern for good, for love, for peace, for justice; but inwardly, Jesus says, they are like ravenous wolves. In the end, many will be devoured by their ideas, either now or in the age to come. Justice without Christ fails.

Moses: Activism That Fails to Bring About Justice

Much of the present justice movement has a theology that is fueled by that which is politically correct. Many workers of justice are motivated only by the plight of human beings, at the expense of connecting with Jesus' desire to establish justice. If the only motivation behind our works of justice is the plight of the people, then we will end up perpetuating injustice in another form.

An example of human justice is Moses before he fled to the wilderness. He grew up wealthy with royal privilege. In Exodus 2, he left Pharaoh's palace and, for the first time, really saw the injustice committed against his own people. Seeing the Hebrews' burden caused Moses to pursue justice in his own strength. We see this same process in the lives of many social revolutionaries. His motivation for activism and revolution was angry sentiment about the injustices committed towards his Hebrew brothers. (Activism, for our purposes, may be defined as pursuing justice in our own power and strength.)

When Moses saw the enslavement of his people, he took matters into his own hands and murdered an Egyptian slave driver. As a result of his rash actions, both the oppressor and the oppressed turned their backs on Moses. The Egyptians wanted to kill him and the Hebrews wanted him to stop meddling (see Exod. 2:11-15). This drove him to the wilderness for forty years, during which time God forged in him the humility necessary for him to become God's appointed deliverer and prophet.

Moses did not have his eyes on the Lord, and was driven by the need of the people, as well as his own anger and sense of right and wrong. He helped no one, and made it worse for himself. James makes it clear: the anger of a man does not bring about the justice that God desires (see James 1:19-20). When we seek to do justice in our own strength, apart from Christ, we will end up propagating the injustices that we are trying to fight.

Various religions and ideologies have started with the plight of the poor, while ignoring Jesus' true agenda for the issue, and they have ended up causing widespread confusion in the earth. False prophets form ideologies and create awareness. False christs are the ones who carry out those ideologies and seek to bring about the reformation.

Islam and Buddhism: False Religions Birthed Out of Desire for Social Justice

Islam began within an unjust society that oppressed women, marginalized the poor, and condoned practices such as slavery and corruption.[3] The founder of Islam, Muhammad ibn Abdallah, was orphaned by age six and felt the sting of being without parents or financial security in the tight-knit familial structure of Arab Bedouin society.[4] At twenty-five, Muhammad married a successful businesswoman. Together, their business prospered, and so did Muhammad's affluence. Despite his prosperity, he did not agree with the lifestyles of the rich merchants who stored up wealth for themselves at the expense of the poor.[5] Muhammad's concern for the poor even extended to his yearly time of retreat, where he would go to the mountains with his family to pray. During these times, poor from the nearby city of Mecca would come to see him and he would distribute alms and food to them.[6]

On one of these retreats, Muhammad had a disturbing spiritual encounter that would ultimately change his life as well as the face of the Arab world forever. The result of this counterfeit visitation was a way of submission, Islam, which purports to call people back to the original message of God, that they create a just society where all were treated equally and with respect.[7] As the downtrodden of society heard this message, they took it to heart, and many of them became followers of Islam.[8]

Buddhism started similarly. A Hindu prince named Siddhartha Gautama, who had never left the confines of his palace, decided to go for a walk one day. There, he saw the plight and dilemma of humanity. For the first time, he saw the sick, the suffering, and the oppressed. Siddhartha abandoned his life of royal privilege, and his wife and young son, to ponder life.[9] He initially endeavored to overcome aging, sickness, sorrow, and death by becoming an ascetic. Seeking enlightenment, Siddhartha deprived himself of food and practiced self-mortification.[10] He eventually came up with a self-imposed religion, a doctrine of demons (see 1 Tim. 4:1-3) that proscribes eight rules for life.[11]

Shimon Bar-Kokhba: A Jewish False Messiah Tries to Overthrow Rome

In the Jewish world specifically, the need for a deliverer has been the catalyst behind many of the christ figures who have appeared throughout history. When Jews began to face pressure in the social, economic, or political spheres, a messiah figure would rise up with a promise of deliverance for the Jewish people. The longed-for messiah was expected to "smite the nations, slay the wicked, and restore the Davidic dynasty, and secondly, [be] a messiah of justice who will usher in an era of peace and harmony."[12]

Following the destruction of Jerusalem in 70 A.D., the Romans continued to oppress the Jews who still lived in Israel. The number of Roman soldiers was tripled, and around 132 A.D. Roman Emperor Hadrian made plans to restore Jerusalem and build a temple. As the Jews began to hear of the emperor's plans, their expectation grew that a promised messiah would appear. Then the Jewish community in Judea was dealt two blows. First, Hadrian's planned temple was revealed to be a pagan place of worship. Second, Hadrian declared an edict banning circumcision.[13]

Rabbi Akiba, the most prominent Rabbi, saw the man he was convinced would lead the Jewish people to victory over their Roman oppressors and declared, "This is the King Messiah."[14] This man, Shimon Bar-Koziba, later called Bar-Kokhba, stepped forward to lead the Jewish people in a revolution against the Romans.[15] The Jews began stockpiling weapons and preparing to take back their land from the Roman rulers. Initially the Jews met with much success, taking up to fifty Roman strongholds in Judea, as well as 985 other towns and villages.[16] Bar-Kokhba set up a Jewish state within Palestine, and the Emperor tried in vain to find an army commander who could bring down the Jewish army.

It finally took the military genius of Julius Severus, as well as thousands of Roman soldiers, to overcome the Jews.[17] After a final decisive battle at Bar-Kokhba's headquarters, the Jewish state was completely destroyed, and the Jews enslaved or sent to other nations. Hadrian banned the Jews from Jerusalem completely and changed the name of Judea to Syria Palestina.[18]

Karl Marx: Proclaimer of an Ideology That Attempts to Bring Social Change Without Christ

Karl Marx was one of the primary formers of socialistic thought, and his legacy has informed the actions of many revolutionaries and reformers throughout the past 150 years. Marx was from a Jewish family but, before he was born, his father had converted to Christianity for social and economic reasons.[19] At a young age, Marx was affected by the poverty and injustice he saw around him.[20] As an adult, Marx rejected Christianity and all religion[21] on the basis that it did not bring about social change at the deepest and most lasting level,[22] but rather lulled people into waiting for a justice that would come eventually in eternity.[23]

"Marxism, it is often claimed, arose in protest against a Hellenized form of Christianity that had forsaken its Jewish roots. In this view Marx was the unwitting heir of the Hebrew prophets who had been submerged and forgotten in a Christianity that had substituted individual piety and mystic absorption for social justice. Christianity, in this view, transferred interest from the proper ordering of society in this world, with which Judaism is concerned, to preparation for another world that promised riches and revelation in the sky as compensation for poverty and pain on earth. The communal, social, and ethical concerns of Judaism, which Christianity had inherited, had been diluted, and even abandoned by an increasingly Hellenized church. Thus Christianity had become the opium of the people and itself helped produce its own antithesis in a Marxism which developed into a kind of secular Jewish messianism—a religion that has its Messiahs in Marx and Lenin, its holy book in Das Kapital, its priesthood in the elite members of the Communist Party, and its kingdom of God in the hoped-for classless society of the future.[24]

Marx wrote many books outlining his philosophies of social justice and revolution, and his ideas have been the catalyst for men and women to take justice into their own hands, sometimes with catastrophic results.[25]

Che Guevara: Attempt to Bring Justice Through Revolution

Che Guevara and his Marxist ideologies are, to this very day, forming the thoughts and ideas of many young people about justice.[26] Ernesto "Che" Guevara began his life as part of a privileged Argentinian family, but from an early age he made it a point to associate with people from all walks of life, both rich and poor.[27] While studying to be a doctor, Guevara and a friend decided to take a journey through Latin America. These travels brought Guevara face to face with the poverty, disease, and hunger of many Latin Americans. Stirred into action, he chose to give up a life of prominence in the medical field,[28] deciding instead that Marxism, which advocated revolutionary overthrows of capitalistic governments perceived to be corrupt and oppressive, was the way to bring social and economic equality to Latin America.[29]

Around this time, Guevara met Fidel Castro[30] and became part of Castro's guerrilla army, which successfully took over the government of Cuba. Guevara took on a leadership role in Castro's regime, heading the war tribunals which led to the execution of at least fifty-five people, but possibly more.[31]

Guevara sustained his strong belief in Marxist revolution as the way to free the oppressed nations of the world, but felt that Castro was not as strongly committed to these views. He left Cuba and found his way to Bolivia, using his guerrilla tactics to try to bring down the government. It was here he was finally captured. Guevara was murdered and buried in a secret location, but his death only increased his status as a martyr and symbol of revolution and social justice. Guevara's influence was apparent in the 1994 Zapatista uprising in Chiapas, Mexico.[32] Chavez, the leader of Venezuela, regards Guevara as "one of his greatest heroes."[33] Evo Morales, on the occasion of Guevara's eighty-seventh birthday, said, "We will never betray the struggle of Che Guevara..."[34]

Jim Jones: Apostolic Socialism Leads to Tragedy

Jim Jones, born in 1931 in Indiana, developed a desire to see racial unity and social change at a young age. By twenty, Jones was buying into the communism expressed by Marx, and headed towards Christian ministry because he felt it was the best arena to draw people into socialist ideologies.[35] Seeing a Pentecostal healing service, Jones concluded that healings, both staged and real, would help to bring people in (along with their money) so that he could do more to relieve poverty.[36] After being rejected from the Methodist church for trying to integrate his services, Jones started another church, which eventually became Peoples Temple Full Gospel Church.[37]

Due to the amount of racism he encountered in the Midwest, Jones decided to move to a more peaceful part of the U.S. Settling in California, Jones became involved in social justice and the politics of San Francisco,[38] hoping to accomplish the social equality he believed in so strongly. Behind the scenes of his organization, however, Jones was preaching another gospel, with 'apostolic socialism' as the central theology and himself as the savior.

> "The Apostolic Socialism of the Peoples Temple fused the communist slogan of Marx's Critique of the Gotha Program with the depiction of early Christian communities in the Book of Acts in which those apostolic Christians held everything in common (Acts 2:45; 4:34-35). Socialism was regarded as the demonstration of divine love, the mathematics of Principle, the workings of God in action."[39]

Jones' doctrine and theology led him to completely reject the God of the Lord Jesus Christ, and to twist Scripture in such a way that he convinced his followers that he was God manifest in flesh.

> "God was translated into socialism; Christ was translated into revolution; and Jesus was translated into justice. When Jones declared himself to be Jesus Christ, fully God and fully human, his claim could be rendered as the assertion that he was the living embodiment of a socialist revolution for justice."[40]

Rather than leading to a social revolution of peace and love, Jones' theology led to the greatest American tragedy until 9/11. Increasingly under scrutiny, Jones moved with almost a thousand members of his community to a piece of land in Guyana, South America, which he named Jonestown. As relatives of those involved in Peoples Temple became more concerned, and with a child custody lawsuit looming over his head, Jones began to prepare his people for what he called "revolutionary suicide."

Finally, on November 18, 1978, after a visit from U.S. Congressman Leo Ryan, Jones decided the time had come for all of the members of Jonestown to lay down their lives for socialism. He sent some members of his community to kill Ryan, while over 900 members of Peoples Temple drank or were injected with deadly poison. Jones died of a gunshot wound to the head. John MacArthur describes the link between Jones and Christ's words in Matthew 24:

> "The greatest tragedy of Jonestown was not that nearly a thousand people died, but that they died believing they were serving God. In truth, of course, they were serving Satan, and were on their way to hell if they did not know Christ…"For false christs and false prophets will arise," Jesus warned, "and will show great signs and wonders, so as to deceive, if possible, even the elect' (Matt. 24:24)."[41]

Justice Without Christ Fails

Justice without Christ fails because Christ is the only one who has made provision and has the power, wisdom, and resources to bring about the inward transformation necessary to redeem society. This redemption comes through living in dynamic agreement with Jesus' ways. Those who live in agreement with Jesus, who live by faith, are the only ones who can labor for the true justice that is in the heart of God. It is this agreement with His ways that Jesus is looking for when He returns (see Luke 18:8).

When Jesus warns us about deception, He is warning us against deception, about the truth of who He is, and the truth of His message. There is no such thing as a deliverer without a message or a movement without ideologies.

Many proponents of and followers of false justice saw the condition of the poor, and they were troubled by it. But in focusing on the cries of the oppressed, they completely missed the cry of the One who would be able to bring deliverance. It is not that we should not consider the plight of the people, but we should not be solely motivated by their condition. Despite their zeal, they were unable to ultimately accomplish justice for anyone, and the ideologies they produced have kept many in bondage to this day. Any attempt to bring justice without Christ will fail.

There is a growing concern for the issues of justice in this generation, particularly arising amongst the media and the entertainment industry. These movements often have the appearance of doing good—they feed the poor and bring humanitarian aid to the needy. However, as these movements are emerging, there are confusing ideologies attached to them. We desire harmony in humanity, but we need harmony with God first. That is the divine order.

Chapter 4

False Gospel

The citizens of Troy watched as the ships pulled away from their shores. Finally, the long conflict with the Greeks was over. The leaders of the city cautiously ventured out into the Greek encampment. The camp was deserted except for a large wooden object in the shape of a horse which stood among the smoldering ruins of the huts and campfires. A young man, Sinon, was found hiding nearby.

Sinon told a convincing tale about being a slave to Ulysses, one of the heroes of the Greek army, and told the Trojans that the Greeks had left him behind as a sacrifice to the gods. When the Trojans questioned Sinon about the horse, he told them that the Greeks had angered a certain goddess, so they built the horse as a gift to her. Sinon convinced them that the horse was left behind to trick the Trojan people into destroying it, which would turn the wrath of the goddess on Troy. Fully taken in by Sinon's story, the Trojans decided to bring the horse into the city. The city of Troy celebrated their victory over the Greeks late into the night.

Once the people of Troy had gone to bed, the truth behind the horse began to unfold. Some of Greece's strongest warriors had been hidden within its frame, and now they snuck out and opened the city gates. Outside the gates, the Greek army was ready in full force, having sailed back under cover of darkness. While the Trojans slept, the Greeks suddenly overtook the city and destroyed it completely.[42]

In a similar way to the Greeks in the mythical story, the enemy is using justice as a Trojan horse within the nations today. Justice is a good thing; therefore, many are unsuspecting and disconnected from the fact that there is such a thing as false justice.

Justice is on the minds of many people. We are living in the twenty-first century, where the consciences of believers and non-believers alike are being stirred concerning the subject of justice. The widespread use of technology, media, and social media at this time in history has connected us to the world around us like never before. As these media and technology outlets have become more and more widespread, awareness of various issues of injustice around the globe has increased. For instance, during the Civil Rights Movement, Americans were alerted to the intensity of what African-Americans were experiencing as their fight for equality was broadcast through radio, newspaper articles and images, and ultimately through the medium of television.[43]

In the U.S., we've seen a rise of philanthropy from professional athletes, entertainers, and executives.[44] Justice organizations are being birthed all over the earth. While it would be nearly impossible to gauge the number of justice-related non-government organizations (NGOs) worldwide, their count has been estimated to be in the millions. In the United States alone, there are more than 1.5 million NGOs, and in India, two million.[45]

Countless websites have sprung up to address the issues of social injustice pervading our modern society: child laborers, child soldiers, human trafficking, blood diamonds, world hunger, environmental concerns, racism, genocide, and many others. In 2006, an Internet search for the term "social justice" yielded 1.5 million hits.[46] Six years later, that number has skyrocketed to 26.3

million hits, showing us just how much more attention this subject is receiving. Starving children are being fed, women are being rescued from sex trafficking rings, and international business practices have been curbed to minimize human exploitation. Overall, many great works are being done by well-intentioned humanitarian workers.

The False Gospel: A False Message of Justice

Addressing the issues of justice is important, but we must be wise and discerning about the various ideologies that are associated with them. There is such a thing as a false gospel or, as Paul calls it, a different gospel. The false gospel is a message that is birthed out of human philosophy rather than the biblical understanding of Jesus Christ (see Gal. 1:6-7). The different gospel is sustained by earth-bound ideas, which interpret truth according to the human situation and experience rather than the word of God. The false gospel makes humanity's definition of right and wrong the foundation of justice, rather than the teachings and principles of Christ. This false message gets our eyes off of Jesus and fosters self-reliance. The false justice message undermines God's eternal plan for justice and goodwill in the world. The gospel of Jesus Christ is the true message of justice. Paul tells us that the true gospel only comes from the understanding of who Jesus is (see Gal. 1:11-12).

The false message of justice, or the false gospel, is man's attempt to establish justice in the world by our own resources, wisdom, and ingenuity. The true gospel of Jesus Christ is not an invention of any human thought. Paul says that he did not preach a gospel that was taught by man, nor did he preach it to please man. The gospel of the kingdom comes from the eternal counsels of the Godhead. In contrast, the false gospel is based on four things: the felt need of man, the opinion of man, the pleasure of man, and the glory of man. The felt need of man because it looks at the immediate need, which in turn fuels these ideas. The opinion of man because it is interpreting truth through the human experience. The pleasure of man because its aim is to please man rather than pleasing God. The glory of man because the false gospel wrongly exalts humanity. It bolsters humanity's confidence that we can bring about our own justice.

I have talked to many young people over the years that have carried very sincere and deep concern for social issues. Some years ago I was with a group of young people dialoguing about issues of social justice and race. During that time I played them a five-minute clip from the movie Malcolm X, which highlighted one of Malcolm X's famous speeches. As they were watching this clip, there was a resounding agreement with the things that he was saying. Once the clip was over, I turned to the Sermon on the Mount (see Matt. 5-7) and began to read. As I read, their hearts were exposed to how much of their paradigm for justice was beginning to be built upon false ideologies rather than the truth of Christ.

On another occasion I was talking with one of these young people, and I simply asked the question, "What does Christ have to say about these issues?" to which they responded, "What does Jesus have to do with this?" This is a response that I have encountered on many occasions when talking about the issue of justice with young people who name the name of Jesus. It is not just that they are actively embracing false ideologies; they find themselves unable to reconcile their understanding of the gospel with social justice. Many young people are more familiar with matters of social justice than they are with the details of the gospel of Jesus Christ. Michael Spencer, in his article, 'The Coming Evangelical Collapse', says,

> We Evangelicals have failed to pass on to our young
> people an orthodox form of faith that can take root and
> survive the secular onslaught. Ironically, the billions

of dollars we've spent on youth ministers, Christian music, publishing, and media has produced a culture of young Christians who know next to nothing about their own faith except how they feel about it. Our young people have deep beliefs about the culture war, but do not know why they should obey scripture, the essentials of theology, or the experience of spiritual discipline and community. Coming generations of Christians are going to be monumentally ignorant and unprepared for culture-wide pressures.[47]

I began to ask myself, "Why is it that sincere believers who name the name of Christ would embrace false ideologies concerning justice?" As I began my search I discovered that a theological vacuum has been created. We have embraced a Jesus who addresses our personal issues and not the issues of society, resulting in two camps.

One camp emphasizes personal transformation at the expense of social justice, and another camp emphasizes justice at the expense of personal transformation. This theological vacuum has created room for the formation of false ideas, shaped by different ones who had a concern for the poor but were not able to find answers in their understanding of the gospel—or the one that was presented to them.

Walter Rauschenbusch

One example of this is the father of the social gospel, Walter Rauschenbusch, whose ideas are still fueling many today. Born in 1861 to German immigrants, Rauschenbusch carried with him a concern for the plight of the immigrant all his life.[48] But it was his first pastorate in New York's rough neighborhood of Hell's Kitchen that opened his eyes to the way the poor lived and died. Rauschenbusch saw that even though men and women found

Christ through his preaching, the injustice of their lives continued on every other level.[49] As Rauschenbusch began to spend time and energy attempting to relieve the daily pressures that the members of his congregation faced, he began to feel that his conversion experience, while real, had been lacking.[50] This awakening to the question of Christian social responsibility resulted in Rauschenbusch writing,

> "Dear friends, there is a social question. No one can doubt it whose ears are ringing with the wails of the mangled and the crushed, who are borne along on the pent-up torrent of human life. Woe to the man who stands afar off and says: Peace, peace when there is no peace."[51]

Rauschenbusch now had a vision for the eradication of not only poverty and inequality, but also the greed and corruption that caused them.[52] As he searched for help to bring together his personal salvation and his social concern, Rauschenbusch discovered a theme within the Bible that seemed to him to be the answer for every part of the human experience—the kingdom of God.[53]

As a writer, professor, and speaker, Rauschenbusch worked towards building a theology for the social gospel. Although Rauschenbusch was sincerely committed to Christ, he felt that some of the doctrines and theological leanings he had grown up with needed to be reexamined. This was a great error on Rauschenbusch's part. The orthodox doctrines of the gospel and the church do not need to be reexamined, rather they need to be extended into the social arena as well by discovering a more holistic gospel as seen in the scripture.

While still in college, he rejected the idea that Scripture was inerrant.[54] He began to preach in subtle ways against the person of Jesus, the atonement, and the reality of eternal punishment.

Rauschenbusch felt that it was unnecessary to emphasize Jesus' divinity.

> "...the social gospel is less concerned in the metaphysical problems involved in the Trinitarian and Christological doctrines. The speculative problem of Christological dogma was how the divine and human natures united in the one person of Christ; the problem of the social gospel is how the divine life of Christ can get control of human society. The social gospel is concerned about a progressive social incarnation of God."[55]

Nothing could be further from the truth. The doctrines of the Trinity and of Christ have deeply profound personal and social implications.

The general tendency is to emphasize these, focusing solely on personal spirituality disconnected from social concern. The answer, however, is not throwing out the basic principles of evangelical theology but rather wrestling with the scripture how orthodoxy translates into social concern and action. We cannot change the gospel to fit our burden for social justice.

When it came to the doctrine of the atoning work of Jesus on the cross, Rauschenbusch felt that every generation had defined the atonement according to its own culture and societal needs, which meant "the fundamental terms and ideas—'satisfaction,' 'substitution,' 'imputation,' 'merit'—[were] post-biblical ideas, and...alien from the spirit of the gospel."[56] Rauschenbusch erroneously dismissed the idea of the guilt of private sins of the world being laid upon Jesus. Instead, he defined Jesus' work on the cross in light of societal injustice, stating that Jesus bore the public sins of humanity, and the way humanity was to enter into the work of Jesus was not by receiving His sacrifice as payment for their private sins, but by entering into Jesus' "realization of God so that they too freely loved God and appropriated his will as their own."[57]

The view of hell Rauschenbusch subscribed to left a little room for punishment of those who had been particularly evil on the earth; but he felt that, in view of God's love, there would have to be a day when those who suffered in hell would have paid the penalty for their sin and would be released.[58]

Rauschenbusch was addressing a very real issue. There are many examples where those who named the name of Jesus were not only silent, but on several occasions participated in various social injustices. Rauschenbusch was reacting to a compartmentalization of the gospel, and in some occasions a hypocrisy, that emphasized personal salvation at the expense of social justice. Instead of integrating both aspects of the gospel, he changed it. Rauschenbusch addressed valid concerns but did so by swinging the pendulum to develop a theology that minimized the sufficiency of the gospel. He did so by undermining the basic and foundational tenets of the faith.

Cleverly Devised Ideologies That Undermine the Gospel of Christ

The apostles regularly warned and exhorted the early church about men who develop cleverly devised ideologies that undermine the gospel of Jesus Christ (see 2 Cor. 11:1-4; Gal. 1:6; Eph. 4:14; Col. 2:8). The apostles, when they were ministering to the early church, often had to plumb line their congregations by reminding them of essentially foundational components of the gospel. These include:

* Jesus' person—His divinity and humanity

* The substitutionary atonement and sufficiency of the cross

* Jesus' physical, bodily resurrection

* The reality of God's coming judgments and eternal punishment

* Jesus' future, physical return to the earth

* The inerrancy of Scripture.

No matter how deep our concern for the poor, these are areas we cannot afford to compromise on. We cannot and must not embrace everything that "screams" justice lest we find ourselves subtly embracing ideas that question the truth of scripture.

The emerging justice movement undermines these truths.[59] The false justice movement continues today in much of the same thought as Walter Rauschenbusch and the social gospel he proclaimed. Different leaders are embracing different versions of the cross, the resurrection, and the physical return of Jesus, as well as the inerrancy of scripture.

Some suggest that the stories of the Bible are not actual events that happened, but rather mere narratives that can be used to gain more wisdom and give a sense of meaning to our lives.[60] Others operate from the premise that the revelation of God in scripture comes from a human perspective rather than divine revelation. This false understanding has led to creating a separation between the Old Testament and the New Testament, where the God of the Old Testament is depicted as angry and that Jesus appeared to change this picture. Rather than seeing the nature of God consistent from eternity and throughout history (Heb. 13:8), they contend that the view of God seen in the events of the Old Testament are seen from a human perspective. Therefore, they argue, the understanding of God, seen in the Old Testament as an angry God is not a true picture of God, but rather a lower understanding of what He is like that would ultimately be abandoned when Jesus appeared to show what God was like.[61] This view is a modern form of Marcionism.

Marcion (85-160 A.D.) was a theologian who was considered a heretic by the 2nd century church. He sought to distinguish between the god of the Old Testament who was angry and the god of the New Testament who was good.[62] Marcion believed that God the Father was not YHWH of the Old Testament.[63] He saw the Father as distinct and superior to YHWH.[64] Therefore, according to this view,

> "The doctrines of the incarnation and deity of Christ are meant to tell us that we cannot start with a predetermined, set-in-stone idea of God derived from the rest of the Bible and then extend that to Jesus. Jesus is not intended merely to fit into these predetermined categories; he is intended instead to explode them, transform them, alter them forever, and bring us to a new evolutionary level in our understanding of God. An old definition of God does not define Jesus—the experience of God in Jesus requires a brand-new definition or understanding of God."[65]

Another leader has called for the need to "widen our parentheses of scriptural orthodoxy."[66] Once the Bible can be interpreted while relying "upon [our] own reason to interpret and apply spiritual truth,"[67] many other parts of scripture begin to be dismissed, including original sin.[68] These same leaders have begun to question the view of the atonement that sees Jesus as taking the punishment for the sin of humanity upon Himself.[69] And finally, they feel that the doctrine of hell leads to "a misunderstanding of the kingdom of God."[70]

True Concern for the Poor Drives Us to Contend for the True Gospel

The true gospel as spoken by Jesus and His apostles was not formed according to the invention of man (see Gal. 1:11-12). Paul's gospel was not rooted in assessing a situation and creating a method to bring about a solution out of human ingenuity. In contrast, the secular justice movement responds to felt needs with humanistic solutions. Jesus states that He was anointed to proclaim the good news of the gospel to the poor. True concern for the poor should drive us to contend earnestly for the faith by laboring to hold the line on the true and holistic understanding of the gospel.

Like the story of the Trojan horse, Jude tells the church that there are certain teachers who are creeping in unnoticed. Paul warns the church of Corinth of the same, telling them that there are false messengers coming into the church, with a different spirit, a different gospel, and another Jesus (see 2 Cor. 11:4). The false messengers Paul speaks of are manifestation of the serpent's attempt to distract the saints from the pure and simple devotion to Jesus Christ (see 2 Cor. 11:3). We must not cast off our discernment for the sake of justice and the poor. Tampering with the gospel is dangerous. We cannot afford to compromise.

Chapter 5

False Worship & Religion

In the island nation of Jamaica, injustice has been propagated for centuries, first through the African slave trade, then through colonialism, and finally through the mindsets that solidified after years of oppression.[71] This former port for the transatlantic slave trade finally gained its independence from the British Empire in 1962.[72] Out of this history, a native-born Jamaican taught a theology that would become the ground from which a new religion would spring up—Rastafari.

Marcus Mosiah Garvey was born in 1887 in Jamaica. Garvey was born at a time when black Jamaicans, who were socially and economically oppressed, were feeling the effects of colonialism in full force.[73] Garvey began to teach that Africans who were displaced throughout the nations, specifically North and South America, needed to unite and repatriate to Africa.[74] This call was designed to restore to black men and women the dignity and self-image that had been taken away through the years of slavery and oppression.[75] Another Jamaican, Leonard Howell, was introduced to Garvey's ideas and in 1933 he began ministering in the slums of West Kingston, Jamaica, preaching Garvey's ideologies.[76]

Howell added a component to Garvey's theology that completely took the message he was preaching out of the construct of Christianity. It had been stated that in 1916 Garvey had prophesied, "Look to Africa for the crowning of a Black King, he shall be the Redeemer."[77] Howell took the crowning of Haile Selassie I[78] of Ethiopia in 1930 to be the fulfillment of this prophecy, and preached that Haile Selassie was "the returned Messiah and Ethiopia…the promised land of all Black people."[79]

Rastafarianism took its name from the name Halle Selassie bore prior to his crowning: Ras Tafari. The new movement grew in significance among the lower classes of Jamaica, who found new self-confidence in seeing themselves as sons of a black man whom they considered to be Christ or God.[80] They rejected the idea that Jesus, through His crucifixion, was the doorway to salvation, seeing in Jesus the white oppressors who kept them socially and economically disenfranchised.

> For Rastafari…the God who these Christian represented did not have the best interests of the poor at heart, and…if the Jamaican underclass—those outside the mainstream who could not afford the canons of respectability demanded by the church—were to have a modicum of respect and dignity they had to abolish the God of the Christians. The Rastas saw very early that one of the main criteria of a God who would help deliver them from Babylon was that this God would have to become one of them.[81]

Now those entrenched in poverty could find their self-respect and dignity in having a God who looked like them. Rastafari was not a religion they joined like others joined the Christian churches.[82] In Rastafari they became part of the movement by rebirth—by becoming sons of Jah, another name for Haile Selassie. Once a Rasta was born into this movement, he changed his way of life.[83] Since Ethiopia was their homeland, Rastas now saw themselves as living in Babylon, and many of the lifestyles they saw lived out around them were part of the Babylonian system. In order to fight against the oppression of Babylon, Rastafarians subscribed to specific ways of living such as vegetarianism and environmentalism. Rastas profess to have a very strong devotion to God,[84] and they use the Bible of the Christians not as a book of infallible truths, but as a handbook to help them interpret history and current events.[85]

The bedrock of Rastafarianism is belief that Haile Selassie is God or Messiah. This is the creed by which they live out their lives. Their identity is strongly bound with the fact that "our deity is African, our prophet is African, our signs and symbols and philosophy are also African. Therefore, to live according to the principles of Rastafari is to live out the essence of an African way of life."[86] Although Selassie died in 1975, Rastas hold that he was God incarnate, and will return to bring them to the "Promised Land" of Africa, specifically Ethiopia.[87]

The Present Social Justice Is Preparing the Poor to Receive the Antichrist

Much like the principles of Rastafarianism, with its worship of Haile Selassie, gave the poor and oppressed of the African Diaspora hope for deliverance, the present social justice movement is paving the way for the poor of the earth to receive the antichrist as God and worship him. This was the point the Lord made to me during my encounter in Mexico City, when He conveyed to me His concern for the poor from a vantage point I never would have expected: *The present social justice movement is preparing the poor of the earth to receive the antichrist.*

His words resounded in my soul and troubled me. His declaration perplexed me. I had never seen this truth until I heard it from heaven. At first I was actually bewildered by that statement and a question rose up in my heart: "How could something as good as taking care of the poor set them up for embracing the leadership of the antichrist?" But I could not deny the fact that it was the voice of the Lord. Afterwards, the Spirit directed me to Revelation 13:16-17. I read the chapter and noticed for the first time that John specifically declared that all would take the mark of the beast, including the poor.

He causes all, both small and great, rich and poor, free and slave, to receive a mark on their right hand or on their foreheads, and that no one may buy or sell except one who has the mark or the name of the beast, or the number of his name (Rev. 13:16-17).

A False Justice Movement Is Emerging in the Earth

Because of this, I began to understand that a false justice movement is emerging in the earth. This movement will seek to serve the poor, but will end up seducing them with lies about the truth of Jesus, leading them into eternal ruin. Multitudes of the poor of the earth will bend their knees before the antichrist and worship the evil one. There is a justice movement that claims to be motivated by compassion to serve and liberate the poor but is, in fact, preparing them to be swept up into something the Bible describes as the mystery Babylon. The harlot religion prophesied in Revelation 17 will serve as a forerunner movement to the antichrist's kingdom. It will prepare the way for the earth, and especially the poor, to receive the antichrist, thus leading them into eternal perdition.

We are living in the beginning of the time frame when Jesus will return to the earth. The scripture makes it very clear that no one knows the day or the hour; however, there are signs given in scripture to help us discern the times and the seasons. When a hurricane develops on the horizon, those on shore can see signs of its impending approach. In the same way, the Second Coming, though glorious, is a great end-time storm (see Amos 1:14), and the Scriptures give us clear signs so that we can prepare for its coming.

Paul gave the church of Thessalonica two very specific signs that must precede the coming of Jesus: firstly, a great falling away from the Christian faith, and secondly, the revealing of the antichrist. He said:

> Let no one deceive you by any means; for **that Day will not come** unless the falling away comes first, and the man of sin is revealed, the son of perdition, who opposes and exalts himself above all that is called God or that is worshiped, so that he sits as God in the temple of God, showing himself that he is God (2 Thess. 2:3-4).

I refer to these signs as two end-time waves. The great falling away is the first wave. This apostasy is deeply connected with the emerging justice movement. Along with its concern for justice, this emerging movement joins itself with any other religion that has concern for the poor, leading to religious syncretism in the name of achieving a greater good for the poor and the oppressed. Although the call to syncretism is increasing, it seems as though many today are more concerned with protesting social injustice than this religious and spiritual compromise.

More than any social issue, the greatest issue in our day is the truth about Jesus Christ: His personhood, His ultimate purpose, and His wisdom to carry out His plan. Deception over these core issues is the driving force behind the great falling away.

The New Testament has much to say about this apostasy. In fact, it is the greatest challenge that is before us in this hour (see Matt. 24:9-13; 2 Thess. 2:3; 1 Tim. 4:1-2; 2 Tim. 3:1-7; 4:3-5; 2 Pet. 2:1-3).

> Then they will deliver you up to tribulation and kill you, and you will be hated by all nations for My name's sake. And then many will be offended, will betray one another,

and will hate one another. Then many false prophets will rise up and deceive many. And because lawlessness will abound, the love of many will grow cold. But he who endures to the end shall be saved (Matt. 24:9-13).

But know this, that in the last days perilous times will come: For men will be lovers of themselves, lovers of money, boasters, proud, blasphemers, disobedient to parents, unthankful, unholy, unloving, unforgiving, slanderers, without self-control, brutal, despisers of good, traitors, headstrong, haughty, lovers of pleasure rather than lovers of God, having a form of godliness but denying its power. And from such people turn away! (2 Tim. 3:1-5)

Satan is using the issue of justice like a Trojan horse to beguile the nations with false ideology. On the outside, it appears harmless, even viable and good, Christ-like; but, it is a vehicle for sowing seeds of deception that undermines the true message of justice found in the gospel of Jesus Christ. In the name of social justice, winds of deceptive doctrine are being devised and propagated by clever and misguided men:

Now the Spirit expressly says that in latter times some will depart from the faith, giving heed to deceiving spirits and doctrines of demons, speaking lies in hypocrisy, having their own conscience seared with a hot iron, forbidding to marry... (1 Tim. 4:1-3).

Unfortunately, many church leaders today are leaving these doctrinal issues unchallenged (see Eph. 4:14) for the sake of the "greater good" of justice. These same leaders are beginning to enter into a view of Christianity that seeks to find common ground with people of other faiths, so that "we would no longer envision a day when all other religions would be abolished and only our own will remain."[88] The pursuit of justice is prevalent in the nations right now. Believers, including church leaders, are laying aside the truths of the gospel for the sake of linking arms around the issue of justice.

Unification of Religions for the Sake of the Poor

Because of this false premise of justice and peace, different ones are seeking to unify the religions of the earth under one banner. Even now, various religions—in particular, the monotheistic religions—are offering olive branches to one another to find common ground for the sake of the poor.[89] But make no mistake: the call for the unifying of the religions under the banner of justice is a doctrine of demons. It suggests that Jesus is offering a peace treaty with demonic forces, condoning their false ideologies while compromising the truth of His heavenly Father for the sake of the poor. The words of the New Testament apostles resound throughout the corridors of history to our day—we must earnestly contend for the faith (see Jude 1:4).

Jesus held the line for truth in His ministry. In John 6, He supernaturally fed the poor, but immediately afterwards challenged the crowd's motives for following Him. He corrected them for primarily seeking Him because of His humanitarian aid, while they failed to pursue Him. In telling His disciples to eat His flesh and drink His blood, Jesus was urging them to break their allegiance with everything else, and lay everything down for His sake. After hearing this costly challenge, John 6:66 says that many deserted Him and followed Him no longer. Jesus then asked His friends, the apostles, a piercing question: "Do you also want to go away?" (John 6:67) Jesus would rather have His best friends desert Him than compromise His character or the mandate of His Father, which is to establish the glory of God and His justice in the earth. Jesus is more than a sympathetic humanitarian.

In the book of Revelation, as the end-time drama unfolds, we see a very similar, troubling thing. The same Jesus of John 6 is now seen as the Lamb who breaks the seals, and the breaking of the third seal causes a famine in the earth.

Jesus Christ is the Just One, and His people are called to witness of His justice in the way they relate to one another and the poor. Our outreach ministries and works of justice must be done through our deep loyalty to Jesus and Him alone. Jesus will not compromise who He is and what He is about. The Spirit is calling for prophetic voices that will call the church to a determined allegiance to Christ and take a stand against the false justice movement that is rapidly emerging in the earth today.

False Justice Movement: Beginning of Harlot Babylon

The false justice movement that is emerging is only the beginning stages of something much more sinister: Babylon, the harlot religion. Revelation 17 is one of the most significant end-time prophecies on this subject. The false justice movement will climax in a one-world harlot religion that will serve as the forerunner to prepare the earth for the antichrist. The Harlot Babylon will be a worldwide syncretistic religion based on religious tolerance and immorality (see Rev. 17:1-6). It will be seductive and deceptive in nature, and its deception will manifest in three arenas: geopolitical, moral, and spiritual.

Geopolitically, the harlot religion will promote justice and peace at the expense of truth. We've seen throughout history, and even just in the last century, that military disputes and social unrest can be deeply rooted in religious differences.

During the ethnic conflict in Bosnia (Bosnia-Herzegovina) from 1992-1995, at least 26,000 Muslims were killed in an effort to separate the various ethnic groups found within the nation.[90]

In 1983 a civil war broke out in Sudan due to increased hostility between Christians and Muslims. Throughout the course of this conflict, the government and the Muslim majority in the north persecuted Sudanese Christians, and over two million Sudanese citizens lost their lives or ended up as refugees.[91]

Northern Ireland experienced internal strife for over twenty years as the primarily Protestant Unionists and the predominately Catholic Irish Republican Army used violence to gain control over the decision whether to bring Northern Ireland into the Republic of Ireland or to remain a part of the United Kingdom.[92]

To avoid future religious hostilities, more and more people are willing to throw away their religious distinctive for the sake of so-called global peace and so-called justice, embracing religious syncretism.[93] Many who are believers in Jesus today will forsake the sound doctrine of the Christian faith in order to promote this ideal of peace (see 2 Thess. 2:3).

Morally, the harlot religion will grow so tolerant of all manner of sexual practices that the sanctity of marriage will be undermined, both doctrinally and legally (see 1 Tim. 4:1-3). Even in the church, unrepentant compromise is increasing, both morally and doctrinally. The false message of grace that goes along with this immorality will seduce many believers. The doctrinal compromise which is also increasing in the church exists in two areas. Firstly, the grace of God is being used for licentiousness—in other words, a justification and a license for sin. This false grace being preached is a grace without repentance.[94] Secondly, many are denying the basic principles of the faith, neglecting key truths pertaining to the nature of Christ and the way of salvation.

The harlot religion will seduce the nations to drunkenness and immorality, impairing their moral judgment and discernment:

> …*"Come, I will show you the judgment of the great harlot who sits on many waters, with whom the kings of the earth committed fornication, and the inhabitants of the earth*

were made drunk with the wine of her fornication."...The woman was arrayed in purple and scarlet, and adorned with gold and precious stones and pearls, having in her hand a golden cup full of abominations and the filthiness of her fornication (Rev. 17:1-2, 4).

Spiritually, this global religion will be wide open to the seductive powers of sorcery and other demonic activities. The Harlot Babylon will deceive all the nations by her sorcery (see Rev. 18:23). Some believers will be seduced by counterfeit signs and wonders which will not be rooted in truth. There is a growing disdain for truth in our society today, and the moment we deny the truth, we open the door to deception. Great delusion is coming to the earth, and the secular justice movement will be a significant part in spreading this delusion like a virus through activism, media, and music.

Music and False Justice

Two twentieth-century examples of this are Bob Marley and Tupac Shakur. Through their music, they espoused a social activist response to the injustice many oppressed minorities and impoverished people experienced. Their message resonated with youth and young adults, encouraging and empowering them to confront societal injustice from a humanistic perspective. Through their influence, many young people joined the false justice movement.

Bob Marley

Bob Marley was born into poverty in 1945[95] in the island nation of Jamaica. During the politically and socially tumultuous period that followed Jamaican independence, Bob Marley's songs brought the injustices of Jamaica and the Third World before the international community.[96] As a social activist, his lyrics appealed to the poor and oppressed. He urged suffering people to take matters into their own hands as the solution to end poverty and injustice.[97] This message of empowerment transcended culture and generation.

Marley's father was mostly absent from early in his life, and Marley and his mother lived in poverty. Ridiculed as a boy for being the son of a white father and a black mother,[98] Marley looked for a sense of belonging, and found it in the ideologies of Rastafarianism. One of the leaders of the Rastas, Mortimer Planno, began to disciple Marley in the Rastafarian way of life.[99] Marley's conversion to Rastafarianism coincided with his rise to prominence in the arena of music,[100] and he expressed the philosophies of Rastafarianism through the reggae music that he would make famous around the world.[101]

Marley's music united people of different backgrounds under the banner of Rastafarian ideologies and put pressure on the unjust systems in Jamaica.[102] Marley and those around him saw themselves not as mere entertainers, but evangelists bringing the good news of Rastafarianism to the world,[103] making him one of the most instrumental proponents of the worldwide acceptance of Rastafarianism.[104] In fact, Marley could be considered the high priest of Rastafarianism. Although Bob Marley died in 1981, his music continues to capture the attention of young people, and the influence of his message of social action continues to grow.[105]

Tupac Shakur

Sixteen years after his premature death at age twenty-five, Tupac Amaru Shakur is still among the world's best-selling rap artists.[106] Born in 1971 to Afeni Shakur, a Black Panther Party activist, Tupac's childhood exposed him to the tough realities of inner city life: fatherlessness, drug abuse, and violence. In fact, Tupac's first rap was about gun control, written in response to the shooting death of a friend.

Tupac's worldview of social justice shaped his music. His experiences growing up in the inner city gave him a hopefulness that existed in tension with the futility and despair of the realities of life in the ghetto. Tupac hoped for peaceable community that was safe for youth, free of killing, gangs, and drug abuse. He desired to affect societal change.[107] Through his music, Tupac raised public awareness of societal injustice and encouraged the social consciousness of youth.

His portrayal of the unjust penal system, police brutality, and racism echoed the sentiment of many urban black young people.[108] Tupac's music spoke of a way of life, and his "thug life" philosophy empowered those from oppressed and impoverished backgrounds with limited opportunity to take pride in making a life for themselves. Tupac justified lawlessness as a desperate, but necessary means to deal with a corrupt societal context.[109] Authors Basu and Lemelle contend that:

> "Since his death, Tupac has become an international martyr, a symbol on the level of Bob Marley or Che Guevara, whose life has inspired Tupacistas on the streets of Brazil, memorial murals in the Bronx and Spain, and bandanna-wearing youth gangs in South Africa."[110]

Due to the appeal of Tupac's message of hope and social justice, presented through his unique and innovative musical style, he has a global following, especially among the youth.

The End-Time Worship Movement Will Confront the Harlot

Satan is using the tactic "goodwill" as the lure to sow deception into the hearts and minds of the nations. He is seeking to prepare the earth to receive him through the person of the antichrist. He is trying to offer the nations counterfeit peace and justice and many people, including believers in Jesus, are falling prey to it. Participating in the harlot religion will inject a culture of spiritual and moral tolerance into the hearts and minds of the nations, thus preparing the way for the earth to worship Satan in the antichrist's kingdom.

The Holy Spirit, however, is raising up a true justice movement fueled by night and day worship and prayer to Jesus, the preaching of His gospel, and the doing of His works of justice among the nations. The end-time church will take a prophetic stance against the harlot by holding the line on truth. This will result in the death of many believers (see Matt. 24:9-10). We will be hated by all the nations.

The leadership of the harlot church will see the true gospel of Jesus Christ as a threat to the "goodwill" they supposedly promote. As a result, these false religious leaders will create government policies that will result in the martyrdom of the saints who are declaring the harlot's demise and exposing her deception. John had a vision of this rampant martyrdom of the saints: *"I saw the woman* [Harlot Babylon], *drunk with the blood of the saints..."* (Rev. 17:6).

The false justice movement insists that, for the sake of the poor, it ultimately does not matter what you believe—that even aside from Christ, what God cares about most are simple acts of goodness and justice. This is a false view and understanding of God. The true gospel teaches us to be fully committed to Jesus alone through faith, love, and obedience to Him. Compromising the truth of Jesus bears an eternal cost. We cannot afford to compromise (see Jude 1:3-4).

The truth of Jesus will greatly trouble the counterfeit justice movement because their definitions of truth, justice, and peace differ from His. Jesus will never agree with the empty principles of the world and self-imposed religion. Jesus is the only way to salvation, and He alone is God (see John 3:16; John 14:6; Acts 4:12; 1 Tim. 2:5; Rev. 7:9). He is the only way to justice, and He will confront both internal and external sin that stands in the way of justice, both now and forever.

The end-time church is the true justice movement, and will be led by Jesus at the head. Jesus is the only One who has the wisdom and power to bring about the justice the nations are longing for. The Lord is calling for true messengers of justice who are filled with deep affection for Jesus and who are committed to doing works of justice and compassion as witnesses of the full justice Jesus will establish when He returns.

We must not yield to the pressure to unify and form alliances with other religions, no matter what the cause (see 2 Cor. 6:14). False religions do not possess the life and the power to transform the human heart. Yet even though the Church cannot agree with other faiths, the scripture calls us to love their followers as Christ does. This love cannot be formed and rooted in human sentiment; Christ and His word, the Bible, must define it.

Although popular culture has made love synonymous with agreement, purporting that we can only love those with whom we agree, this is not true. God loved unbelievers without compromising Himself (see John 3:16). We are to seek the well-being of every person, and we need to see their dignity and treat them with respect (see Matt. 5:45). We must be tender, yet also faithful witnesses to the truth.

While a movement may look good on the outside, if it is not Christ-centered, it cannot ultimately produce the justice that God desires. In fact, the biblical understanding of Jesus is the litmus test of whether a justice movement is true or false. Setting our hearts on Jesus should be central to our pursuit of justice. Knowing Christ by walking with Him in intimacy and growing in a biblical understanding of Him will powerfully influence how we understand justice.

As we seek to do works of justice and compassion, we must grapple with how to integrate social justice with the true biblical understanding of Jesus Christ. We must take a stand and hold fast to the truth of Christ, and we should have His preeminence in our hearts above any social issue that concerns us. We must pursue justice with an undying allegiance to Jesus. Our works of justice must be done His way and on His terms. This justice, in the name of Christ, is an expression and exaltation of Him, and glorifies His Father.

Part II

TRUE
JUSTICE

Chapter 6

Global Worship Movement for Justice

In February 2008, Exodus Cry, a ministry that seeks to raise awareness and end human trafficking through concentrated prayer and works of social justice, was praying for Cambodia during their weekly Monday night prayer meeting. Here's what they testified that night:

> One of the singers on the worship team began to prophesy in song over Cambodia, "Freedom is coming! Freedom is coming! Freedom is coming!" There was an unusual anointing and energy upon this phrase as he sang it. We could all feel the truth and power of this prophetic declaration.[111]

Arriving home late that night after the prayer meeting, one of the leaders of Exodus Cry opened his email inbox to find an email from a friend in Cambodia, explaining how he had felt led to go to a certain area of town where there were many brothels. Driving by the brothel-filled area:

> He felt the Spirit well up within him and he began to declare, "Freedom is coming! Freedom is coming! Freedom is coming!"[112]

The two friends started comparing the two time frames, and the leader of the Exodus Cry team realized that the declarations had been made from the United States and Cambodia at the same time. After this encouraging exchange, though, the human trafficking situation in Cambodia continued without evident change. Exodus Cry asked the Lord weekly for raids on brothels that would bring freedom to those in forced prostitution in Cambodia.

The Exodus Cry leader shared:

> "Week after week nothing seemed to happen. I was frequently asked if maybe we should focus our prayers in a different direction, but I truly felt impressed that we were confronting a stronghold in the spirit and we just needed to stay steady. Many times I shared that I felt we were on the verge of a large breakthrough."[113]

Then, at the beginning of May 2008, Exodus Cry heard from their friend in Cambodia that forty-eight brothels had been closed and 255 of the workers freed. This happened within the very same area he had been driving in the night two months before when, an ocean apart, he and the singer had proclaimed, "Freedom is coming!" over Cambodia.

This testimony from Exodus Cry demonstrates a powerful truth—prayer and worship are part of God's strategy to bring forth justice. Jesus continues to work for justice on the earth today as He lifts His voice before the throne of God, crying out in intercession (see Isa. 53:12; Rom. 8:34; Heb. 7:25). He is also lifting His voice through His people in the ministry of intercession and proclamation.

Jesus' Primary Strategy to Establish Justice: 24/7 Worship and Prayer

Jesus' primary strategy to establish justice in the earth is by calling His people to a global 24/7 worship and prayer movement (see Isa. 62:6; Jer. 31:7). The issue of justice is established in the eternal counsels of the Godhead, the Trinity, from before the foundation of the earth. Robert Kyser states that the Trinity is a divine "community of single action."[114] The execution of God's plan is Trinitarian. The Father has specific plans in His heart for good, peace, and hope (see Jer. 23:18; 29:11). The scripture declares that the Father has appointed Jesus to carry out the Father's plan (see Ps. 2:6-7; Isa. 42:1; Matt. 26:39; John 4:34; Heb. 10:9).

The Son of God executes the Father's eternal plan for justice through the Holy Spirit (see Isa. 11:1-3; 42:1-2; 61:1; Luke 4:18). The primary way that Jesus administrates the Father's plan is by declaring the Father's intent, which releases the Holy Spirit's activity. We can see this principle at work in the very beginning. The scripture declares that God created all things *through* His Son (see John 1:3; Heb. 1:2). Jesus as Creator was intimately involved in the Genesis 1 process (see Prov. 8:22-31; Col. 1:16) by speaking the Father's word, *"Let there be light"* (Gen. 1:3).

Not only did Jesus speak the Father's words, He Himself is the Word. A word is that which gives expression to thoughts, ideas, and feelings.[115] Jesus is the Word of God because he carries out the Father's plan. He leads His Father's kingdom, holds together the universe, leads our lives, and combats the enemy by speaking the Word of God (see Matt. 4:3-10; Col. 1:17; Heb. 1:3; James 1:18; Rev. 19:13). Jesus' administration of the Father's plan through speaking His word serves as a model of how the saints partner with God's plan in the world.

The power of God's Spirit is released when the Father's words are spoken through intercession or worship (see Eph. 6:17). There are two powerful realities behind the various injustices in the nations of the earth: 1) men making real evil choices from a depraved heart and, 2) demonic forces. Both of these dynamics necessitate the release of the power of God to bring about eternally lasting transformation in the world. We can create laws, which will bring restraint, but the Lord is after that against which there is no law—the full manifestation of God's glory and character in every sphere of society, which is the fruit of the Spirit (see Gal. 5:22-23). Only the Spirit can break through the powers of darkness (see Eph. 6:12) and the darkened heart and minds of men (see 2 Cor. 4:4-6). These hearts and minds are confronted by the preaching of the word of the gospel of Jesus Christ, while the powers of darkness are driven back by the declaration of God's word in worship and intercession.

Jesus the Messiah is the premier social reformer and He requires night and day prayer for justice in the societies of the world (see Luke 18:7-8). We do not only pray and worship; we are also to be engaged in doing works of the kingdom such as evangelism, feeding the poor, healing the sick, and discipleship. Intercessory worship, though it seems weak in the natural realm, is the primary means and the most powerful weapon that God has chosen to establish justice in the earth (see 1 Cor. 1:27-29). Prayer is our primary work (see Luke 18:1; Col. 4:12; 1 Thess. 5:17). Prayer is a legitimate and practical expression of concern for the oppressed. It confronts the invisible forces of darkness behind injustice and releases the activity of the Spirit to establish justice in society as well as the inner life.

The pursuit of justice must start in the place of prayer. There are demonic forces in the earth that can only be confronted by prayer, and there is injustice in our own souls that can lead to the perpetuating of injustice if it is not confronted in the place of prayer. Prayer not only changes the spiritual atmosphere in our cities but also of our souls. It increases the presence of God in our hearts and deepens the agreement with Christ in our hearts which is necessary for transformation.

How would the life and impact of Muhammad, Siddhartha, Marx, and others have been different had they willingly engaged with the God of Jesus Christ and inquired of Him (see Ps. 27:4) instead of seeking to bring justice in their own strength? Prayer delivers us from our own ideology, sentiments, and perspective by aligning our hearts with God's. Through prayer, we can receive God's perspective on the issues of the day and the people involved—both the oppressed and the oppressor.

Interacting with God through worship and prayer strengthens our faith and encourages us in times of weariness, especially during the times when the issues we are focusing on seem to turn for the worse. Prayer connects our hearts with the One who is not discouraged. Prayer brings us into deeper fellowship with Jesus, protects us from self-righteousness, powerfully transforms our hearts, and releases the power of the Spirit in our lives as well as the issue that we are contending for. Intercessory worship is the greatest weapon we have for the release of justice and it is a force that cannot be stopped.

The New Song: The Song of God's Administration

In Isaiah 42:10-12, Isaiah prophesies various details of what God will do to establish justice in the earth, and the Lord commands His people in the nations to sing the new song to God and worship Christ.[116] The new song is the song of God's administration in the earth, and through prayer and worship, Jesus leads His people into agreement with His heart. In prayer, we come into agreement with God's plan. In worship, we come into agreement with who God says He is. As we agree with Jesus, He manifests His justice in the earth.

In Luke 18:7-8, Jesus shows us that night and day prayer and justice are deeply linked to each other:

> *And shall God not avenge His own elect who cry out day and night to Him, though He bears long with them? I tell you that He will avenge them speedily. Nevertheless,*

when the Son of Man comes, will He really find faith on the earth?

In this passage, Jesus uses the plight of a widow as the context to teach about night and day prayer, which suggests that God's vision for justice through prayer is not only spiritual, but social as well. The prayer movement will bring about a historic breakthrough of the Spirit resulting in God's justice in the earth.[117]

Scripture declared that God would raise up a night and day prayer movement as the end of the age approaches:

> *I have set watchmen on your walls, O Jerusalem; they shall never hold their peace day or night. You who make mention of the Lord, do not keep silent, and give Him no rest till He establishes and till He makes Jerusalem a praise in the earth* (Isa. 62:6-7).

The concept of night and day ministry to the Lord is born of divine initiative out of the holy heart of God.[118] In small but growing ways, this is already a global reality. Within the last twenty years, the Lord has been birthing prayer initiatives and movements from small groups of believers, resulting in societal impact. There is also an increase of large prayer and worship events being held across the nations of the earth.

Prayer and Worship Events

TheCall, a grassroots prayer movement, held their first solemn assembly on September 2, 2000, gathering on the The Mall in Washington, D.C. TheCall DC had over 400,000 youth and young adults in attendance crying out to God for revival and national issues with prayer, fasting, and repentance. Since then, TheCall has held numerous corporate prayer meetings where thousands gather for twelve hours of worship, fasting, and repentance as a response to the prophetic call in Joel 2:15-18: "Declare a holy fast, call a sacred assembly, bring together the elders, gather the children."[119]

In the United States, the National Day of Prayer is held on the first Thursday of May each year. The National Day of Prayer Task Force states their mission is to "mobilize prayer in America and to encourage personal repentance and righteousness in the culture." In 2012, millions observed the National Day of Prayer.[120]

Prayer and Worship Ministries

In addition to these one-day prayer assemblies, the Lord is raising up many prayer and worship ministries across the earth. Some serve daily for several hours and others have 24/7 prayer.

Middle East

In Turkey, a Muslim-majority nation of 70 million people, young adults are founding houses of prayer, and the church has doubled in size in the past ten years. Youth prayer initiatives are also emerging in Lebanon and Syria.[121]

Australia/Oceania

In January of 2006, Tauranga House of Prayer in New Zealand was birthed by a small group of young adults committed to daily prayer.[122] In the Solomon Islands over two decades ago a believer in Christ was fasting in the jungle when the Lord told him He would raise up His house of prayer in every nation, tongue, and tribe. In March 2009, this word began to be fulfilled as a Solomon Island jungle village of about 200 residents began the Fa House of Prayer. It has continued in 24/7 prayer ever since.[123]

Africa

In Nigeria, E.A. Adeboye led all-night prayer meetings in 2001 with 4 million intercessors in attendance. A month later, a

Christian president was elected. The last decade has seen a rapid growth of Christianity in Nigeria. In 2010, another Christian president was elected. Every month, millions in Nigeria gather to pray for their nation in an all-night prayer vigil.[124]

South America

In Brazil, Before the Throne ministry records a live worship album with two million attendees each year. Night and day prayer is growing across this nation, and the church has increased from 15 percent to 30 percent in the past decade.[125]

Anticipando in La Paz, Bolivia began in 2000 with a few prayer meetings a week. Through various internships and their school of prayer, they have trained and equipped many to live a lifestyle of prayer and fasting. They currently have 48 two-hour prayer meetings each week.[126]

Europe

24-7 Prayer is a Britain-based international and interdenominational ministry that has birthed prayer furnaces in over one hundred nations worldwide since it began in 1999.[127] Since the first student-led prayer meeting, unceasing prayer has gone forth from this prayer, mission, and justice movement. 24-7 Prayer advocates for intercession for social justice, as well as actively pursuing works of justice from the place of prayer. In Ukraine and Russia, prayer movements are emerging as well.[128]

North America

At the International House of Prayer in Kansas City, Missouri, unceasing prayer and worship has continued since September 19, 1999, twenty-four hours a day, seven days a week. The International House of Prayer in Atlanta, Georgia was founded in 2004. Though it started with forty weekly hours of prayer and worship, since February 12, 2006, night and day prayer has gone forth from this Atlanta-based house of prayer.[129]

Since 2007, the Luke18 Project has been equipping college students to establish prayer furnaces on every college campus in America. To date, over four hundred such gatherings have been established.[130] In January of 2010, 24-7 Prayer launched a new initiative called Campus America to establish prayer rooms on all 2,614 U.S. college campuses.[131]

Injustice Confronted Through Prayer

As the Godhead brings natural history to its climactic end, transitioning the nations into the age to come, Jesus will establish justice in every sphere of society in the nations. Global prayer will culminate with the return of Jesus to establish His throne on the earth and fully manifest the justice of God.

One of the primary ways that Jesus is going to confront social issues such as social oppression, human trafficking, ethnic hostility, the AIDS crisis, and the war on drugs will be through His church globally engaging in night and day worship and prayer.

At the International House of Prayer in Kansas City, Missouri, I am part of a leadership team in the NightWatch that gives oversight to 250 young adults who pray and worship before the Lord each night from Midnight to 6 a.m. One night in 2010, Chris Tofilon, a NightWatch worship leader, had just returned from a ten-day prayer trip to Ciudad Juarez, Mexico. This trip had been organized in response to the corruption, violence, and injustice of the drug cartel turf wars which had put Juarez on the map as the murder capital of the world.[132] A group of believers from both Mexico and the U.S. had come together to seek God's justice in prayer.

During the trip, pastors from Juarez stood at the border of Mexico and the United States, praying that God would end drug trafficking, break the control of the drug cartels, and open a door to revival and transformation in the region. On October 18, three days after returning from this trip, Chris prayed in the Night-Watch for Juarez, asking the Lord to bring power to the church and to change the spiritual atmosphere in that city. Sada Rogers, another leader in the NightWatch, remembers joining in prayer for Juarez that night:

> "The thoughts of hopelessness that had bombarded my heart and mind over the past few months in regards to Juarez and the seemingly countless news reports I had heard of murders, mass murders, and unchecked crime began to come over me. I then checked those feelings against the truths found in Acts 4, looking at the God who made the heavens and the earth, the sea and all that is in them, and was reminded that turning the situation in Juarez around was not impossible…with one word from His mouth, He created the heavens, so with one word from His mouth, He could drive darkness far from Juarez, and make them a city of light. So that's where I prayed from in contending for Juarez's current trauma and her destiny."[133]

God heard the heartfelt prayers of believers and responded. Within hours, CNN broke the news story that the largest drug bust in history had happened in Tijuana, Mexico in the early morning hours that same day. Authorities seized 134 tons of marijuana and detained eleven people. These drugs were being trafficked by the Sinaloa Cartel—one of two major drug cartels primarily responsible for the violence in Juarez.[134]

Prayer in Abolition: Exodus Cry

Exodus Cry has many testimonies of praying for a specific city and seeing major trafficking busts in that region within just days or weeks of their weekly prayer meetings. For the entire month of May 2010, Exodus Cry targeted the pimp culture in prayer, asking the Lord to expose its brutality and bring justice. Two days after the month ended, a dramatic human trafficking bust was made in Brooklyn, New York, and gang members were charged with running sex trafficking rings and recruiting girls from junior high schools.[135] Prayer is not a spiritual side point to the works of justice to Exodus Cry—it is an integral part of how God delivers human beings from modern-day slavery.[136]

Just as Exodus Cry seeks to abolish human slavery in the 21st century, imagine for a moment a new Underground Railroad movement, where abolitionist centers across the earth pursue justice from a place of worship. These centers would have abolitionists who daily give themselves to the worship of Jesus and ask for His guidance. Harriet Tubman was an abolitionist who walked in the spirit of prayer. Her faith and intimacy with Christ fueled her abolitionist efforts. As a woman of continual prayer, she often received prophetic revelation from Jesus of where and how to rescue slaves.[137]

Like Harriet Tubman, modern-day abolitionists who follow Christ can take a stand against the avalanche of organized crime and perform great exploits to rescue trafficked boys and girls, bringing them into the place of worship. These centers will be filled with believers who seek His face in intercession and worship.

When we pray to the chief abolitionist, Christ Jesus (see Isa. 42:7), and inquire of Him in prayer and through the word, it strengthens us to see His divine strategy and how to move forward in our efforts to bring justice to the nations of the earth (see Isa. 42:4).

Community Centers and Night and Day Prayer

In 2008, while on a ministry trip to Seoul, Korea, one night I had a dream that I was in an inner city in the U.S., feeling the weight of God's presence and fear of the Lord. I was standing in front of an outdoor basketball court filled with children, and I could hear their happy and playful voices. While this was happening I couldn't help but think of Zechariah 8:4-5:

> *Thus says the Lord of hosts: "Old men and old women shall again sit in the streets of Jerusalem, Each one with his staff in his hand because of great age. The streets of the city shall be full of boys and girls playing in its streets."*

This scripture was strongly impressed on my spirit. As I continued to think about it, I realized that the scene before me of children playing in the inner city was a picture of these scripture verses. I knew that there was coming a time when the presence of Jesus would be released in the inner cities, making them a safe place for boys and girls to play.

As I was standing there, I looked to my right and found myself next to a community center. This center had night and day worship and prayer to Jesus taking place, alongside mentoring programs, sports and recreation, counseling, and after-school tutoring—all the things that normally take place in community centers.

Suddenly, I had an open vision while still in my dream. In this vision, I saw community centers with night and day prayer being established in various inner cities in the United States. I saw these prayer-and-worship-fueled community centers spreading across the country, and I heard a voice say, "inner city monks." When I heard this phrase, I knew that these justice workers would be like the Franciscan monks who, as lay people, gave themselves to prayer, fasting, and works of justice. I understood that there would be social workers who were followers of Christ, committed to justice in the context of fasting and prayer. I believe this is possible through the grace of God.

Why Worship and Prayer

True justice begins with our restored relationship and agreement with God in Christ. One of the primary ways that we connect with God is through worship and prayer. God always intended to bring about His purposes in agreement with humans through Christ. As we engage in night and day prayer for justice, our hearts come into greater agreement with Him, and we grow both in prayer and in doing His works of justice in the earth.

There are many reasons that we should engage in daily worship and prayer as followers of Christ. First is simply that prayer and worship is agreement with God, joining in with what He wants to do in the earth. Second is that in worship and prayer we can enjoy the nearness of God's presence (see James 4:8). Third is that in the place of prayer and worship, angels and demons are moved, changing the spiritual atmosphere of the cities we are praying for (see Dan. 10:10-21). Fourth, God's government is manifested and administrated through worship and prayer—it is the way He runs His kingdom forever (see Ps. 22:3). Finally, it is through worship and prayer that the Holy Spirit releases His power for the works of justice in and through His Church (see Joel 2:15, 28; Luke 24:49; Acts 1:8; Acts 4:29-31; Acts 13:1-2).

The night and day worship and prayer movement which God is raising up in the nations is itself a justice movement. Believers who have a vision for the kind of justice Jesus desires must fuel their labors of justice and compassion with worship and intercession. Not every person, nor every ministry, is called to 24/7 worship and prayer—but Jesus requires prayer and worship in His church. It is one of His premier strategies to establish justice.

Prophetic Singers and Musicians: Message-Bearers of Jesus' Justice

In contrast to the popularity of artists like Bob Marley and Tupac, who advocated a man-centered social justice, Jesus is raising up singing prophets and musicians who give their allegiance to Him. Through the Word, Jesus wants to share His thoughts and His feelings about injustice (see Isa. 59:15) so that these singing prophets and musicians can be effective message-bearers of God's justice through their music. This music will be powerfully anointed by the Holy Spirit, and these songs will instruct the church and the nations concerning the glory of Jesus and His plan to bring justice to the earth.

In Isaiah 6, Isaiah sees Jesus' glory and hears the seraphim speak of His beauty and vision for justice, which is the whole earth being filled with the glory of God. This heavenly scene causes Isaiah to be filled with the fear of the Lord (see Isa. 6:5). Later, in Isaiah 24, Isaiah sees the glory he saw before God's throne now being released on the earth through the church. This glory fuels the prophetic song: "Glory to the Righteous One" (Isa. 24:16),[138] and produces in Isaiah the same response as seeing the manifest glory of God: "Woe is me!" (Isa. 24:16).[139]

Singers and musicians who have a concern for justice must be connected with God's vision to fill the earth with His justice. Their hearts must be aligned with the truth of Jesus' ways so that they can proclaim His glory and beauty to the earth through the new song.

Chapter 7

The Gospel: The True Message of Justice

The book of Acts recounts the following story (see Acts 21:15-22:21). Paul had finally made his way back to Jerusalem, bringing with him Trophimus. Then, one day, while Paul was in the temple, the allegation arose among the Jews that he had taken Trophimus, who was a Gentile from Ephesus, into the temple.

There was tremendous racial animosity between the Jews and the Gentiles at that time, and this animosity was reflected in various areas, including the place of worship. Within the temple was a wall of hostility.[140] Written on it was a warning:[141] "No Gentile may enter within the barricade which surrounds the sanctuary and the enclosure. Anyone who is caught doing so will have himself to blame for his ensuing death."[142] Another area where this hatred manifested was in marriages between Jews and Gentiles. The Jews were so opposed to these that if a Jewish son or daughter married a Gentile, they sometimes performed a funeral and considered them as good as dead.[143]

Once the accusation against Paul was noised across the city of Jerusalem, it caused a great disturbance. This led the Roman centurion in that city to intervene. The commander put Paul in chains, and as he was about to take him away, Paul addressed the angry crowd. The crowd became silent and listened as he began to tell his testimony. Paul shared about his past as a Pharisee of Pharisees, and how his zeal for the law culminated in obtaining letters that gave him permission to kill and imprison believers. Paul spoke of the journey he made to Damascus to do just that, and of the face-to-face encounter he had with Jesus along the way. He recounted his meeting with Ananias, who shared with him the good news of Christ's offer of forgiveness to Paul, and spoke of his calling as an apostle to the Gentiles.

Most people in this situation would have ended their testimony there and given the altar call. Yet Paul continued, "Jesus said to me, *'Depart, for I will send you far from here to the Gentiles'*" (Acts 22:21). Enraged, the Jews tore their clothes in anger and Paul was taken back into custody by the Roman centurion.

Why would Paul make that point? Why was Jesus' command for Paul to go to the Gentiles pertinent to the situation at hand? After all, it was the hostility between Jews and Gentiles that got him into that situation to begin with. What did Paul's testimony of his personal salvation have to do with the social climate that was charged with racial tension?

When Paul later writes to the Ephesians we find out that it had everything to do with the gospel. Paul shares with the church of Ephesus that Jesus did not only come to save our individual souls, but also came to break down racial barriers—the wall of hostility (see Eph. 2:14). Paul had a holistic picture of the gospel that addressed both the need for personal salvation and the transformation of society.

The Gospel of Jesus Christ Is the Message of Social Justice

In our pursuit of social justice, there is a temptation to compartmentalize social justice from the gospel. The tendency is to think of the pursuit of justice as one thing, while our understanding of the gospel is something entirely separate. Focusing on the gospel is focusing on justice. Many believers today are in search of a unique message or are looking in all the wrong places for insight pertaining to the issue of social justice. The reason for this is that much of what is proclaimed in the pulpits at large is a gospel that is disconnected from its social implications.

This is the issue that many of the false social reformers encountered. Some met with a church and a gospel that was disconnected from social issues and, therefore, not robust enough to truly challenge the problems of society. The true gospel of King Jesus and His coming kingdom is the only message for us today. If our understanding of the gospel is not far-reaching enough to address all things pertaining to life—including our own society—humanistic ideas and our favorite political perspectives will creep in to fill a theological vacuum.

I was faced with similar difficulties as a young believer as I sought to understand how my faith addressed all areas of society. For the most part the faith that I was exposed to solely presented a personal understanding of Jesus. A personal understanding of Jesus alone is insufficient to address issues of social injustice. By itself, the message of being taken away to heaven is not strong enough to confront the issues that the poor and oppressed deal with.

Jesus and the apostles of the early church did not see the message they were preaching in this compartmentalized way. For them, there was only one message: the gospel of Jesus the Messiah and His kingdom—a government that rules by principles of righteousness and justice. Our hope is not just to be in heaven but to be in God's just society on earth forever.

Our understanding of the gospel is profoundly affected by the picture we have of Jesus (see Gal. 1:10-11). This is why it is crucial that we have a proper, biblical, and complete understanding of who Jesus the Christ is. He does not change according to the times, and neither does His gospel, which is entirely sufficient to address all areas of life (see Heb. 13:8; 2 Pet. 1:3).

Jesus Is the Messiah

One day Jesus came to His disciples with a most important and heart-piercing question. *"Who do men say that I, the Son of Man, am?"* (Matt. 16:13). When the eternal Son of God asks a question it is important to note that He is not asking because He needs information—He is putting us on a road of discovery. The disciples answered and gave Jesus the various answers and opinions about His identity that were being spoken around Israel. These statements made one thing clear: the crowds did not have clarity about who Jesus was.

After the disciples answered Jesus, He made the question more personal: *"Who do **you** say that I am?"* (Matt. 16:15, emphasis added). He was asking if they were clear about His identity. The same is true today. There are many opinions about who Jesus is and what He is really about. The Holy Spirit today is asking the church the same question that was asked of the apostles over 2000 years ago.

The Bible declares that Jesus is the Christ (see Matt. 16:16-20). The Holy Spirit wants to give the church a holistic understanding of what it means for Jesus to be the Christ or the Messiah so that the church can have a holistic understanding of the gospel. The Messiah was one who was expected to bring Israel into the messianic age (see Acts 1:6), remove injustice, and establish God's righteousness and justice so the glory of God's justice would fill the nations of the earth. His mission was to establish *shalom*.

> *"...precisely because of Israel's status within the purposes of the creator god, **Israel's king was always supposed to be the world's true king.** 'His dominion shall be from one sea to the other; from the River to the ends of the earth'*

(Ps. 72:8). *'The root of Jesse shall rise to rule the nations; in him shall the nations hope'* (Isa. 11:10, cited Rom. 15:12)...What the Gentiles needed and longed for, whether they knew it or not, was the Jewish Messiah, who would bring the just and peaceful rule of the true God to bear on the whole world."[144]

According to the scripture, the time around Jesus' birth was a time of messianic expectation (see Luke 2:8-14, 25-32, 36-38). Many were ready for Israel to be delivered once and for all from the social and political oppression of the Gentiles. The Messiah was the answer to their social and political freedom (see Luke 2:38). When Jesus came the first time, though He addressed various social issues, He also was very clear as to what the purpose of His coming was, which was to deliver Israel from herself; i.e., her sin (see John 8:31-36).

This was a large source of offense for the nation. In many ways they were on the opposite end of the spectrum of many believers today. Israel saw the Christ as a socio-political deliverer, while many believers today see Him mostly as a personal deliverer. The angel Gabriel told Joseph that Jesus would deliver people from their sins (see Matt. 1:21) and set up a just socio-political infrastructure (see Luke 1:31-33). The Messiah, Jesus, is both a personal and socio-political deliverer.

The Gospel Calls for the Transformation of Souls

For the new and just society to last, a new nature must be given to its citizens and future leaders of the new world (see John 3:3, Rom. 8:17; 1 Cor. 6:2; Heb. 2:5; Rev. 5:10; 20:6). During His First Coming, Jesus came to lay the foundation for this new society from heaven that will be established on the earth (see Matt. 7:24-25; 1 Cor. 3:11; 2 Tim. 2:19). He came to remove the primary source behind social injustice (see John 1:29). The gospel of Jesus Christ is a religious and a political announcement. It calls for the worship of the true and living God and it puts the leaders of every sphere of society on notice that there is a change coming (see Rev. 14:7).

When we rightly understand what the gospel is, we will see its clear agenda. The gospel calls for the transformation of souls, which leads to the formation of redeemed men and women who pursue right social action to establish justice in society.

In Jesus' day there was tremendous hostility between the Jews and the Samaritans. It is believed that the Jews did not walk through Samaria at all. Jesus addressed this issue in a very well-known story—the story of the Good Samaritan (see Luke 10:25-37).

A lawyer one day approached Jesus to test Him, by asking Him what he must do to obtain eternal life. Jesus answered the lawyer by asking him about the law of God and his interpretation of it. The lawyer recited the first and the second commandment, *'You shall love the Lord your God with all your heart, mind, soul and strength,' and 'you shall love your neighbor as yourself'"* (Luke 10:27). Jesus proceeded to tell the teacher of the law that his answer was correct and that following through on this would lead him to eternal life. However, the lawyer got defensive and asked a most revealing question, *"Who is my neighbor?"* (Luke 10:29). Jesus answered his question by telling him the story of the Good Samaritan.

I have often heard this story as an exhortation to show compassion to those in need. There are very powerful humanitarian applications found in this story, but that was not the primary reason why Jesus told the story. There are two important keys to understanding this powerful story. We must connect it to the historical backdrop of the Jewish-Samaritan relationship and we must keep in mind that Jesus is telling the story to answer the question, *"Who is my neighbor?"*

The point of Jesus' story was made clear by the lawyer's answer to Jesus' question—the Samaritan was the neighbor. Whereas the second commandment is often thought of in terms of loving people in our ministry spheres and maybe even other ministry streams. Jesus is confronting racial and social barriers—love the Samaritan as you love yourself.

We need a true message to plumb line the church as the primary agency of social justice in the earth. This same message will raise the oppressed and the oppressor out of the ash heap of their personal depravity, putting them in the pathway to receive the fullness of deliverance when Jesus returns in the resurrection (see Ps. 113:7-8; Matt. 5:3-5). As a result of compartmentalized presentations of the gospel, many people try to emphasize either the internal or external aspect of the gospel over the other. Jesus, however, wants to deliver the oppressed from both.

Faithful Ambassadors of the Gospel

Much of what is known as the gospel today is really only the introduction to the gospel—the message of forgiveness and the born-again experience. The gospel is much broader than this alone. The gospel that Jesus and His apostles proclaimed included forgiveness. But in its entirety, the gospel is the message of justice that comes from God's government being established on the earth because of the finished work of the cross. The gospel of the kingdom is the declaration of God's entire plan, administered by Jesus Christ, for all of created order and society.

The proclamation of the coming kingdom of God is the hope for all of the redeemed, but in particular, for the poor and the marginalized who are in Christ (see Luke 6:20). For them, it is good news because it contains information about God's plan to bring inward transformation, as well as His plan to bring social justice to the earth (see Luke 4:43; Luke 8:1-2). The church must become faithful ambassadors of the gospel, which is the only true message of justice. We must not succumb to the humanistic philosophies that are fueled by human sentiment and earthbound theological perspectives. We must be ambassadors of Christ who represent His message and agenda for the world.

Because my father was a diplomat in the foreign services, I was given a chance to see what the life of a diplomat is like. This is on the forefront of my mind when I see Paul calling himself an ambassador of Christ (see 2 Cor. 5:20; Eph. 6:20). In many ways, as believers, all of us serve as ambassadors of Jesus, and this word picture gives us insight into how we ought to live as we do the works of our King and His kingdom. An ambassador is appointed by the king or president of their nation to represent him in another country as the highest-ranking diplomat. In this sense, Paul really was an ambassador, because Jesus truly is a King.

As ambassadors of Christ, we represent a King who rules a kingdom that will be brought forth on the earth in fullness. Ambassadors must have their primary loyalty to the king or government of the country in which they are citizens. Traditionally, ambassadors are sent to a foreign country for a short term. This is to prevent them from having their affections compromised by living in a new culture for too long. Though Paul lived on the earth, he spoke of having citizenship in heaven (see Phil. 3:20), and living in such a way so as not to be conformed to this world, its basic principles, and philosophies (see Rom. 12:2). We must let our actions and values be shaped by the kingdom of God, not by this present age.

Additionally, ambassadors do not have the right to change policies or negotiate terms set by the government they represent. They cannot simply ignore national policies or make them more palatable to the nation in which they are doing their diplomatic work. All an ambassador can do is present the terms. If there needs to be any changes in the terms, they need to be discussed with the broader government he or she represents. Paul, as ambassador, was given the gospel decree from the King of Kings. Paul was unashamed of this message (see Rom. 1:16) and stood firm on it to the end. This decree is the same one we carry out today.

We only have authority to declare what the gospel says. An ambassador of Christ does not have the prerogative to change God's terms according to their opinion or the opinion of the people they are trying to reach. We have not been given the right to "improve" or edit God's divine decree. We only have authority to declare what we have been told to declare. As ambassadors, we must fear Jesus regarding His gospel. If we tamper with it, as His messengers, we will be in danger of both temporal and eternal judgment (see Gal. 1:6-9; Rev. 22:18-19).

Paul says that even if an angel were to present another gospel, that one would be in danger of judgment (see Gal. 1:8-9). The gospel is an entrustment (see 1 Thess. 2:4). God has not commissioned us to see a need and adopt a message based on that perceived need. We must be motivated by the understanding of Jesus and the Word, not by human opinion. It is important that we give ourselves to prayerfully experiencing Christ's presence, which is the only way to come to more fully understand His gospel (see Gal. 1:15-16). When we do so, this understanding of the gospel becomes our motivator to address justice and not our own opinions, agendas, or the need of the people.

As an example of this, Paul wrote to the church in Rome about the justice issue of anti-Semitism. When we read his letter carefully, we see that he was not motivated by human opinion. Even though he was a Jew, he was not writing out of a sense of patriotism or of being personally wronged. He viewed the entire issue in light of the glory of God. The first thing to notice is that Paul begins talking about Israel immediately after writing about the vastness of the love of Christ (see Rom. 8:38-39).

When Paul addressed this issue, he was moved to do so from a place of prayerful encounter. From there, he proclaimed that when he talked about Israel, he was speaking the truth in Christ (see Rom. 9:1). He was not moved for Israel because he was a Jew. As a matter of fact, he would explain in another letter how the Jews, his own countrymen, had been the source of some of the greatest trials in his life (see 2 Cor. 11:26). Something else was operating in Paul's heart—the manifestation of the personhood of Christ Jesus in every sphere of society. We need this same motivation if we are going to represent Christ in the earth. If we are going to be His ambassadors to the forgotten and rejected, to other nations and cultures that are not like ours, then we must be like Paul who speaks the truth of Christ, unmoved by personal preference.

When we have experienced the love of Jesus, we become messengers for His sake, like Paul did. Paul's zeal for Israel wasn't for his own sake, or even for Israel's sake; he cared about Israel for the sake of God's name and His glory throughout the universe. Our desire to preach the gospel to the destitute and downtrodden of the earth—to establish justice—should be primarily for God's sake. It should be for His glory first, and for the well-being of the people second.

When speaking to the Corinthians, Paul further explains the role of believers as ambassadors: *"For we do not preach ourselves, but Christ Jesus the Lord, and ourselves your bondservants for Jesus' sake"* (2 Cor. 4:5). By this, Paul means that we do not preach our own agendas, the platform of our favorite political party, or anything that showcases us. We do not preach to impress others. We preach to see Christ established in the hearts and minds of others.

The gospel is a serious issue; it is a subject that is near and dear to God's heart. Paul asks: *"For do I now persuade men, or God? Or do I seek to please men? For if I still pleased men, I would not be a bondservant of Christ"* (Gal. 1:10). A bondservant of Christ is one who is fully surrendered in love to the Man Christ Jesus, committed to His cause. As bondservants of Christ, we must understand God's intent for people in contexts like racism, poverty, human trafficking, abortion—in any and every pertinent context—and speak His word concerning it as found in the Bible. We aim to please an audience of one—the Man Christ Jesus—and we seek to see Him established in the hearts of the nations. To the measure that the emerging social justice movement falls short of the gospel is the same measure that it is driven by the fear and perspectives of man rather than the fear of God.

God's ambassadors represent Christ Jesus and His agenda for justice in the earth. As Christ's messengers, we must take a bold stand for the faith of Jesus Christ and His apostles (see Jude 1:3-4). Again, this is about our paradigm of justice, rather than our methodology. Of course we want to address the tangible, practical needs of the poor and oppressed. In fact, that is part of how they will become open to hearing what we have to say. But once that door is opened to us, we must preach Jesus. Neither the needs of the poor nor the voice of our culture should shape our understanding of the gospel.

If this concept of "preaching Jesus" sounds clichéd to us, it exposes how little we know Him. The Jesus Paul encountered was so magnificent in His splendor that Paul needed the Spirit's help to speak of Him (see Eph. 3:8). The Spirit is calling messengers and workers of justice to experience the glory and splendor of Christ in such a way that all they can do is talk about Him. When we touch this experience, we will need the Holy Spirit's help to rightly speak of what we have seen and heard.

The call that is before every cultural prophet is to preach the majesty of the Man Christ Jesus and His vision for justice, which includes the full establishment of justice in the coming ages. When it comes to pursuing social justice, we need to understand that the subject of justice is all-inclusive. We are not representing any political party. We are not representing any social status: middle class, poor, or wealthy. We are not representing any ethnic group: white, black, Hispanic, Chinese, or Korean. And we are not representing any gender. We are representing the Lord Jesus Christ, speaking on behalf of His heart concerning whatever the issues might be.

When we preach the gospel to marginalized people, we are calling them to set their hearts on the majesty of Jesus, sharing with them the good news of His plan of salvation. The vision of God's great eternal plan and hope for the earth—the promises that refer to the end of the age—will fuel the poor and the oppressed to live out the central exhortation of the Sermon on the Mount, which is to seek first God's kingdom.

The Sermon on the Mount is the King's instruction to the oppressed on how to walk out their lives in the context of oppression. And it is the guaranteed method to actually dismantle injustice. If we want to be more than activists—prophets and deliverers—we must connect the oppressed with these world-changing truths of the kingdom of God. Justice is not only highlighted by the prophets in the Old Testament. Even in the New Testament, the subject of justice lies at the very core of the good news of Jesus Christ as proclaimed by Himself and His disciples. The establishing of justice is central to both the First and Second Coming of Christ. In the Word we see that there is no separate message for justice. There is only one answer: the gospel.

The Proclamation of Christ Is the Way Forward

The proclamation of the gospel of Jesus Christ is the way forward. Faith in Christ is primary in this battle, and out of true faith comes the works of God. This is not to say that we should not be concerned about providing humanitarian aid—we should be. Scripture requires that we do works of justice, such as healing the sick; driving out devils; freeing captives; advocating for fair business practices; confronting the evils of society such as racism; and feeding, clothing, and sheltering the poor. Outside of faith in

Christ Jesus, all of our humanitarian aid has no eternal value. It does not matter how well intentioned someone is in their philanthropy or advocacy for social changes. If they are outside of faith in Christ, their works do not have lasting power to establish the justice on the earth that Jesus desires.

Before the throne of God, unbelieving humanitarians will find that their works are burned as nothing (see 1 Cor. 3:12-13). These works will carry no merit in the court of heaven. Yet people of faith who do works of justice in the name of Christ make a greater and more lasting impact than the combined efforts of the earth's billionaires. Giving someone a cup of cold water in His name matters in a real and eternal way to those who love Jesus.

What do we do, then? In our thinking we must lay a proper foundation of Christ while contending for justice in the way that Christ would have us contend for it. If we do, the Lord will give us results that will powerfully witness to the nations before the Lord returns. His church will heal the sick, feed the hungry, deliver the demon-possessed, and care for the fatherless and the widow.

Our outreach ministries and works of justice must be done through our radical commitment to Jesus and Him alone. Jesus will not compromise who He is and what He is about. The Spirit is calling for prophetic voices that will call the church to a determined allegiance to Christ and take a stand against the false justice movement that is rapidly emerging in the earth today.

We need workers of justice. But God is calling forth more than people who can carry out good deeds, even as much as that is needed. He is raising up forerunners—men and women who are filled with the understanding of the gospel and who move in the power of God as they do His works of justice in the earth. The One who loves justice is calling for people to join with Him in His zeal to make the wrong things right, and to bring His good news to those who are in desperate need of both social and spiritual deliverance.

The Spirit is raising up an end-time justice movement that will exalt Christ. We have a divine invitation to join Him in His holy desires and to take a stand for justice, both in our own souls as well as in our society. All we must do is set our hearts to understand and agree with His ways and to pursue His solution—that in all things, Christ may have the preeminence.

Chapter 8

The Messiah: Jesus, the Just One

In my early years as a believer, I was taught foundational truths about Jesus. I firmly held onto these truths: Jesus is fully God and fully man, born of a virgin, and all His words and deeds as recorded in scripture are true and trustworthy. His death provided the atonement to cleanse those who accept the gift of His payment from all sin, and He was resurrected on the third day and ascended into heaven. The reality of Colossians 1:18, that Christ would have preeminence in all things, became a goal that, along with the other believers in my life, I am continually seeking to grow into.

However, the disconnect between my clarity on a doctrinal level and my activism on a social level became more clear to me in the conversations I had with a group of students at Southeastern University, the Bible college I attended. These students carried a strong desire to see justice come to the poor and oppressed of the earth, and I discussed with them about how Christianity connects to social justice. I was alarmed, however, by the way in which they went about making this connection biblically. As others have done in the past, in their zeal to show a Jesus who was connected with the plight of the poor, they actually undermined the Jesus that I knew from the Word. For them, it seemed that the pursuit of justice led them to call into question the nature of Christ, His mediation, His resurrection, and His deity.

I strongly disagreed with their liberal theology, and told them so. But the points they brought up concerning Jesus as the defender of the orphan and widow opened my eyes to see that, while all I knew about Christ up to that point was true, I had a compartmentalized understanding of Jesus and His plan to redeem the earth.

As I studied the verses they brought to my attention (most were found in the Old Testament) I saw that the cross of Christ had not only paid for the sins of the earth on a personal level, the cross was actually the inauguration of a kingdom ruled by Jesus, the King who cares deeply about justice coming to the earth. I began to see that Christ was not only to have leadership in all things pertaining to my personal life and salvation, but all things concerning society and creation. Jesus, the Just One, will have the supremacy over humanity as well as all of the cosmos.

The Splendor of Jesus Must Be Central to Our Pursuit of Justice

The Word states that the splendor of the Man Christ Jesus is preeminent in the heart of God and, therefore, must be central in the discussion and pursuit of social justice. This is the primary thing on the heart of God (see John 17:1; Phil. 2:10). Colossians 1:18 draws attention to the reality that Christ will have preeminence in all things. This verse has both personal and societal implications. The plan of God is that His Son should have preeminence in every sphere of life.

> *And He is the head of the body, the church, who is the beginning, the firstborn from the dead, that in all things He may have the preeminence* (Col. 1:18).

As Paul states to the church of Colossae, "all things," must include every area of society and, therefore, our efforts for social justice. It is in the Father's plan of redemption to see Christ's pre-eminence in marriage, education, environment, and other spheres of society. When the subject of the preeminence of Christ comes up, for some the issue of social justice is not naturally what comes to mind. This is due to the fact that much of our perspective in our Christianity is often limited to our own personal lives, because we have a compartmentalized understanding of who Jesus is.

A more complete understanding of who Jesus is includes the reality that when Jesus returns, He will not only come back to gather the saints in the rapture, but also to establish justice in every society of the earth. The Second Coming has profound implications in the addressing of urban crime (see Zech. 8:4-5); revolutionizing the ethics of international trade (see Isa. 60:5-6); restoring and preserving the environment (see Isa. 11:6-9; 41:18-20; Ezek. 47:8-9); emancipating slaves and prisoners of war (see Isa. 42:6-7; 42:9; 49:8-12; 61:1-3); eliminating racial hatred (see Isa. 2:4; Eph. 3:6; Rev. 7:9); putting an end to human trafficking (see Joel 3:3); and many more tangible issues of social justice.

At Jesus' Second Coming, He is not only coming back to take us to heaven but to bring heaven to earth and fix the environment. David declares that when Christ returns He will come as a defender of widows and a father to the fatherless (see Ps. 68:5, 146:9; Prov. 23:10-11).

A Biblical Understanding of Christ Is Essential in Our Pursuit of Justice

One of the main reasons this false justice movement is arising in the earth—as well as why so many believers are buying into it—is because we have not embraced the full Biblical understanding of what it means for Jesus to be the Christ and that He will be leading a true justice movement at the end of the age. Scripture is very clear about the spiritual, political, and sociological implications of Jesus being the Christ. Now, more than ever before, we need to look at the full counsel of God related to what it is that Jesus was about.

Salvation, for the most part, has been limited to the cleansing of the heart and forgiveness of sins, divorced from its social implications. We need to see salvation encompassing not only the renewing of man's heart, but also the renewing of society and the earth. In fact, though Jesus talks about being born again, the message of the gospel is not just a born-again reality. The born-again experience is what gives us entrance into the kingdom of God. It is not just a mystical kingdom; it is a heavenly kingdom that comes to the earth.[145] When Jesus returns, He is not coming to rescue believers from the planet, but to establish a new society in the world.

Additionally, many people respond to the poor's cry for justice as the basis for which they do justice. This response is still compartmentalized, however, because the poor and oppressed do not know what they are really crying out for. All they know is that there is something terribly wrong. But far from dismissing this cry, God takes it very seriously. He is the Author of justice. He loves justice.

The truth is that there is a strong global vision in the heart of the Father to establish justice. Isaiah the prophet shows God's response to the deceitful oppression of the day as well as the moral decline. He displays two powerful emotions concerning the earth's lack of justice: zeal and displeasure. It displeases Him that there is no justice (see Isa. 59:15), and He is clothed in zeal (see Isa. 59:17). The word, ra'a, which Isaiah uses for "displeasure," includes the connotation of having one's heart shattered to pieces.[146]

God is not a passive observer of injustice. His heart breaks every time a young girl is taken captive by traffickers. His heart is shattered into pieces every time a baby is aborted. He is not merely spectating; He zealously desires to establish justice on the earth. Yet even as we touch how deeply He is moved over this, we need to understand that He is not simply reacting. He is not scrambling to fix what is broken. He is a just and a wise Judge (see 1 Tim. 6:16), and from eternity He has a clearly devised plan to establish unceasing justice in the world.

Beloved, we must earnestly fight for the biblical understanding of Christ. The true crisis in the nations today that is greater than any form of social injustice is the lack of the understanding of Jesus Christ. We must have a full, Biblical understanding of who He is if we want to see biblical justice go forth on the earth. The good news is that the Holy Spirit wants to speak to us about these things. He wants to tell us about God's heart and God's plans if we take the time to read His Word, talk to Him, and listen to what He has to say. Integrating social justice with the true biblical understanding of Christ is essential. The truth of who Jesus is must be preeminent above all the issues we may be concerned with.

Isaiah 42: The Father's Vision for Justice

Isaiah 42 details the Father's vision for justice. I encourage anyone who cares about the subject of justice to become very acquainted with this chapter and make it a regular part of their study, meditation, and teaching. A framework for understanding this chapter includes:

* 42:1-4 God's vision for justice

* 42:5-9 God's partnership with His Son for the release of justice

* 42:10-12 The global worship movement for the release of justice

* 42:13 The Second Coming of Christ to establish justice in the earth

The vision for justice lies deep within the heart of God. God is the God of justice; He loves and requires justice (see Mic. 6:8); He will bring forth His vision to establish justice on the earth.

When the Father reveals His vision for justice, He starts by drawing our attention to His Son:

> *Behold! My Servant whom I uphold, My Elect One in whom My soul delights! I have put My Spirit on Him; He will bring forth justice to the Gentiles* (Isa. 42:1).

Jesus is the One who will bring about the fullness of the justice that is in God's heart. The Father's declaration in Isaiah 42:1-4 is one of the clearest prophetic statements concerning His vision for justice. The Father highlights seven aspects of Jesus that reveal His purpose, His power, and personhood, emphasizing how necessary it is that we possess a Christ-centered perspective of justice.

"Behold My Servant Whom I Uphold"

God is committed to ending injustice in the earth. Before anything else, the Father calls us to behold His Servant as part of His strategy for establishing justice. The beholding of Christ or a deep devotional interaction with Jesus is essential. As we interact with Christ through the Word, He convinces us of His vision and strategy for justice, as well as His commitment and ability to see it accomplished in all of society. The Father directs those who are crying out for justice to turn their attention to the Son of God. The Father is calling us to have a determined focus on Jesus that takes precedence over all other issues.

There is a biblical principle that we become like that which we behold (see 2 Cor. 3:18).[147] Based on this principle, if we are preoccupied with the injustice, rather than being preoccupied with

Christ, our hearts will grow discouraged by the weightiness of the injustice. Focusing only on the felt needs of the people perpetuates the problem, locking us within human sentimentalism. We can start to become jaded, cynical, and bitter. We must remember that the cry for justice is birthed first and foremost in the heart of God, and it is the governing principle of His kingdom.

For this reason, being devotionally preoccupied with Jesus in prayer is vastly important. As we set our hearts on Christ, we will become convinced not only of power to establish justice, but also His wisdom to do it. When we experience these things about the Man Christ Jesus, it will sustain our hearts and strengthen us in times of weariness and discouragement.

Jesus calls us to wait for Him until we discern His heart for justice. Walking humbly with Him is central to our pursuit of justice. As we grow in our Biblical understanding of Christ, we are empowered to take His message to the poor and oppressed of the earth. If we truly connect with the Just One, then justice will flow like a river (see Amos 5:24).

The Father's first priority is to reveal His Son (see John 17:1). We see this priority demonstrated at Jesus' baptism. At that time, Israel had received no direct word from God for four hundred years. Many scholars refer to the time period between the book of Malachi and the start of the New Testament as the four hundred years of silence. Yet the first time the Father spoke, breaking centuries of prophetic silence, He had this to say: Look at My Son. "… This is My beloved Son, in whom I am well pleased" (Matt. 3:17). This is especially striking in light of the cultural context of the day.

The Roman Empire—the current dominant world power— was rampant with immorality, which shaped the moral climate of the first century. Many injustices were being broadly accepted as societal norms: slavery, forced relocation of people from their native lands, gladiators, governmental corruption, homosexuality, idol worship, gluttony, incest, fornication, and adultery, just to name a few. And this is the society that received God's first audible words in four hundred years.

He could have said, "Away with crucifixions." "Away with the gladiator system." Or even, "Away with the gluttony of Rome. Let's change the over-indulgent culture of wasteful feasting." The Father could have said any one of those things and more, because they were true, and they did need to be removed. Yet His first words were not related to societal reform—or so it seemed. Rather, He gave a command to behold His Son Jesus.

God's approach throughout Scripture is consistent. Before He calls us to address the issues, He draws our attention to Christ (see Exod. 3; Isa. 6, 42, 61; Jer. 1; Ezek. 1; Matt. 3; Rev. 5). The Father's commitment to the Man Christ Jesus is a paradigmatic foundation for our understanding of the issue of justice. Everything the Father does in history by His power is for the vindication and the glorification of His Son.

The Father declares that Jesus is the One He upholds, which means that He alone is the One whom the Father endorses. Jesus has the Father's backing—all of His support and His resources—to do His job as God's Servant, the King of the whole earth. The Father is clear: when we behold His Son Jesus, we see that He is the One endorsed by God.

"My Elect One"

Jesus is the Elect of God first in that He is the full and complete revelation of God. All of God's actions and statements are communicated through the Person of Christ. In Jesus, God's revelation of Himself is complete because Christ is God's decisive word to humanity.

The writer of the book of Hebrews tells us that God has revealed Himself to our fathers at various times and various ways through His prophets. What sets Jesus' revelation of God apart from the prophets is that He is God Himself. The uniqueness and finality of the revelation of God is found in His beloved Son Jesus Christ. When we look at Jesus, we see exactly what the Father is like. Jesus alone can reveal the splendor of the Father, because He is the exact representation of God's character. Looking at Jesus through the Word is the only way to discover how God thinks and feels about justice and what His action plan is (see Heb. 1:1-3).

Jesus is God's Elect One as God's appointed heir of all things (see Heb. 1:1-4; Ps. 2:6-7). The scripture tells us that Jesus is the heir of God's vast empire. Because of Adam's rebellion in the garden, humanity lost dominion over the earth. The Man Christ Jesus recovered that dominion through His death, burial, and resurrection, through which He received all authority in heaven and on earth from His Father.

The divine appointment of Christ as heir of all things is in regard to Jesus' humanity. Calvin says, "The name 'heir' is attributed to Christ as manifest in the flesh, for in being made man and putting on the same nature as us, He took on Himself this heirship, in order to restore to us what we had lost in Adam."[148] The Godhead already possesses all things (see Ps. 24:1), but being the heir of all things is God sharing His fullness with the Man Jesus Christ.

Jesus' leadership is now only seen in part (see Heb. 2:8) but will be revealed in full when Christ returns (see Eph. 1:9-10) to establish God's just and divine society on earth. Jesus is God's chosen King who will administrate God's justice and government in all nations of this world. All the nations will come fully under Jesus' leadership in the coming age (see Isa. 42:1-4; 1 Cor. 15:25-28; Rev. 11:15-18).

"In Whom My Soul Delights"

Before God talks about His strategy to establish justice, the Spirit calls us to the most magnificent subject, which is the Father's delight in His Son. Beholding the Servant of the Lord—or in other words, pursuing the Biblical understanding of Jesus Christ—includes seeing and connecting with the Father's delight for His Son (see John 17:26).

The realization of the Father's affection for Jesus causes us to heed and obey the Son of God (see Matt. 17:5). The Servant is God's minister of justice and is the delight of the Father's soul. His character, nature, and works please the Father fully (see Col. 1:19). The Father's own glory is reflected back to Him through His Son, Jesus. As we begin to touch the truth of this divine delight, we ourselves grow in love for Jesus as the Just One and feel what the Father feels towards His own Son as He administrates justice. In this way, justice begins by touching the Father's delight for His Son. When we understand the Father's vision for justice, and His commissioning of the Man Christ Jesus to bring about justice, we can participate in full partnership with Him to bring true justice to the earth.

"I Have Put My Spirit upon Him; He Will Bring Forth Justice to the Gentiles"

Jesus has been given the Spirit without measure (see John 3:34). The Spirit being put upon Him affirms that He is God's appointed servant. He is Christ, the Elect One. The Spirit being upon Jesus also speaks, however, of the supernatural resources that are at His disposal to accomplish and administrate God's justice in the nations of the earth (see Isa. 11, 42, 59, 61; Rev. 5:6).

God has given this Man, the Just One, a mission to establish justice in the nations of the earth by His Spirit. Jesus' ability to bring justice to all the people groups of the earth is supernaturally empowered by the Holy Spirit (see Isa. 11:1-3). There is tremendous power that the Father has bestowed on His Servant (see Eph. 1:19), as well as divine authority (see Eph. 1:20-21; 2:6).

And Jesus came and spoke to them, saying, "All authority has been given to Me in heaven and on earth. Go therefore and make disciples of all the nations, baptizing them in the name of the Father and of the Son and of the Holy Spirit, teaching them to observe all things that I have commanded you; and lo, I am with you always, even to the end of the age" (Matt. 28:18-20).

In the Great Commission, we see God's desire to share this power and authority with His people as we go through society as workers and messengers of justice (see Matt. 28:18; Acts 1:8): It is from the power and authority of the Spirit upon Him that Jesus sends out His disciples to do His works. True justice can only be established by the supernatural power of the Holy Spirit (see Zech. 4:6).

This is not to minimize the value of human participation in raising awareness through means such as websites, documentaries, flyers, and music; but on their own, none of these efforts are enough. As our awareness is raised, we must stay in the place of intimate interaction with the Servant Jesus through prayer. It is there that we see His supernatural power and ask Him to release it on the earth. He alone can bring justice to the nations.

After He had commissioned His disciples, Jesus told them to wait in Jerusalem until they had been endued with the power of the Holy Spirit (see Acts 1:8). Though Jesus already had a plan for justice, and had even already appointed His followers for the work, He told them first to wait on the Lord in prayer. One hundred and twenty of them did, and it was out of that place of prayer and supplication that they received the divine empowerment that Jesus had promised. Starting with the very first workers of justice in the New Testament, the mission of justice began with prayer, unto the release of the activity of the Holy Spirit in and through the Church.

"He Will Not Cry Out nor Raise His Voice"

Jesus will not cry out nor raise His voice, nor cause His voice to be heard in the street (see Isa. 42:2). What this means is that Jesus is not going to mobilize people to protest, nor will He form a militia to accomplish His cause. He is not going to lead a demonstration down the street in revolt, as many activists and revolutionaries have done. Forming a militia and organizing noisy protests is not His method. Neither is it His way to lead a march. Even in the midst of the oppression of the Roman Empire, the only march that Jesus did was along the Via Dolorosa, carrying the cross (see John 19:17). His methods concerning justice are not like other men.

When Jesus spoke on the earth at His First Coming, His voice proclaimed the kingdom of God; but rather than doing so through campaigns or rally cries, He proclaimed His agenda for justice through the gospel and confirmed it with power, signs, and wonders. Jesus has much to say about justice, but His methods are not like other men.

"A Bruised Reed He Will Not Break and Smoking Flax He Will Not Quench"

Jesus will establish justice through the gentleness of wisdom. He will not break a bruised reed; He will establish justice through divine gentleness. This is a prominent theme throughout this section of Scripture: Isaiah prophesies that though fierce in His judgments, Jesus will confront the idols of the earth through His humility and gentleness (see Isa. 42, 49-55). Jesus is going to confront every false god and every humanistic ideology by demonstrating the glory of His humility.[149] His unique meekness is one of the very things that set Him so far apart from any other god. The God of justice is the uncreated One who clothed Himself in the garments of humanity and revealed Himself as the Servant of all. This is forever what He is like, including when He overturns injustice on the earth.

God is going to confront the darkness of the nations of the earth through His humility, and one of the main ways He will do this is by displaying His humility in and through His bride, the Church (see Ps. 149:9). This means that our destiny is to become a humble, just people. At the end of the age, He wants to form humility and servanthood in our hearts as we partner with Him for the unfolding of His glory among the nations of the earth. As workers of justice, we must pursue the divine gentleness that Christ embodies. Like Micah says, as we do justice we are to walk humbly (see Mic. 6:8).

Describing Christ's method of justice, Isaiah continues, "smoking flax He will not quench" (Isa. 42:3). This is a vivid prophetic picture because it takes precision to be able to blow on a spark, bringing it into fuller flame, without putting it out. Here, Jesus takes smoking flax—a wick of a lamp that barely has a spark—and He turns it into a raging bonfire of justice. It requires great skill and patience to nurture that smoking flax, turning a dimly burning wick into a spark, and then fanning it into flame. It is with this wisdom that God will establish justice in the earth. The whole earth right now is like smoking flax, a dimly burning wick, a place where justice is hardly found (see Isa. 59:15). Yet Jesus will nurture it until the fires of justice He desires consume the planet (see Luke 12:49).

"He Will Not Fail nor Be Discouraged"

"[Jesus] *will not fail nor be discouraged, till He has established justice in the earth; and the coastlands shall wait for His law*" (Isa. 42:4). As we behold Jesus we see His holy determination to see justice established in the earth. One of the reasons Jesus is not discouraged is because God's plan for justice was established in eternity past (see Job 42:2). Justice was birthed within the eternal counsels of the Godhead.

When our works of justice are fueled by human sentiment and political agenda, this can lead to impatience and frustration. But if our vision for justice is fueled by God's plan for justice and our interaction with Him through Christ, Jesus will impart His resolve, wisdom, and divine gentleness to our spirit. In understanding His desires for justice, we become confident that He will bring it to pass.

If we behold only the injustice—the ebb and flow of circumstances—the times of breakthrough and setback may make us feel like we aren't making progress at all, and as a result, discouragement sets in. This is why it is important for us to behold Jesus. When we behold Him instead of the issues, our hearts get strengthened with hope as we see His resolve. Jesus is going to end injustice in the earth forever, and He is filled with confidence that He will accomplish this.

Jesus is not discouraged by the widespread injustice in the earth, even though He feels intense pain about it. Many believers are connected mostly with the pain of injustice, and as a result burn out in their ministry efforts. We need to follow Christ's example of holding two things in tension: the present pain of injustice, and our future hope that true justice will be established, and that all injustices we currently see will be corrected. We need to learn how to carry our burden in the present, like Jesus does, knowing that our hearts are stewarded and sustained by our hope in the certain future of justice.

We steward the burden of the Lord by our confidence in His ability to establish justice. Jesus says,

> Come to Me, all you who labor and are heavy laden, and I
> will give you rest. Take My yoke upon you and learn from
> Me, for I am gentle and lowly in heart, and you will find

rest for your souls. For My yoke is easy and My burden is light (Matt. 11:28-30).

Jesus calls us to exchange our burden for His. This means that we must carry His concern for justice, rather than our own, because His pain over injustice is holy and pure, while ours is broken and dysfunctional. He sees perfectly; we see in part. He is not discouraged, but we are easily discouraged. So when we behold Him, and thus take His yoke upon us and learn from Him, His burden will become our sustenance.

Beholding Jesus, the Servant of God, helps us to resist the temptation to become cynical and weary in our hearts when we see injustice. Through our intimate fellowship with Jesus, we connect with both the intense pain the Lord feels about injustice, as well as His determination and confidence in His own ability to orchestrate justice on the earth. Otherwise, all we have is our own pain, and over time, that only produces negative feelings in our own soul such as weariness, discouragement, and depression. We must be confident that Christ possesses divine resolve and holy zeal in His heart for justice.

Chapter 9

Jesus, the Man of War

Beholding the Servant of the Lord will give us insight into the method He will use to establish justice in the earth. In Isaiah 42:10-12, the Lord calls for a global worship movement from among the nations. The end-time justice movement is a prayer movement. We are called to lift our voice and cry out in the place of prayer first (see Luke 18:7), and proclaim the gospel in the context of living lives of doing justice (see Mic. 6:8; James 1:27).

As singers proclaim the glory of Jesus, He will respond in power to bring justice to the earth. When the new song goes forth, the vision in the heart of the Father to establish His justice for all eternity is brought to pass—Jesus Christ returns to earth as a mighty Man of war in response to the prayers of His people to defeat the perpetrators of injustice.

The parable of the persistent widow regarding night and day prayer is in the context of the injustice in the end times (see Luke 17:22-18:8). What is perhaps most unexpected about this parable is that it ends with a question: will faith be present in the earth when Jesus returns (see Luke 18:8)? At first glance, this question may seem disconnected from the rest of the story, until we understand that though we are laboring for justice through prayer—and have some measure of impact on the world today—the fullness of the justice God desires will be released on the earth when Christ returns.

The Second Coming is a vast subject, and is often trivialized, because many believers consider this subject irrelevant, thinking of the Second Coming only in terms of an escapist paradigm that expects Jesus to return to take us away from this planet. Yet Jesus is not coming to take us away, but to set up His Father's kingdom and establish justice here on the earth. Next to the death, burial, and resurrection of Christ, the Second Coming will be the most glorious event in human history.

The Second Coming will openly manifest the extent of the justice that was accomplished at the cross of Christ. The events surrounding the return of the Lord are the most mentioned in the word of God. There are at least 150 chapters in the word of God focused on the subject of the end-time activities of God.

The study of the end times has powerful implications to living lives of faith and doing the works of the kingdom in the present. The apostles regularly called the early church to live lives of obedience to Jesus and faithfulness to His purpose. There are at least a hundred occasions the apostles use future glory to address present issues.

The return of Jesus to the planet will be the great revealing of the face of Christ as the Bridegroom, King, and Judge. Jesus will come back, set up His government in Jerusalem, and manifest His full leadership over all the kingdoms of the earth and every sphere of society (see Ps. 2; 24; 110; Isa. 2; 11; Jer. 3:17; Rev. 11:15). If we are going to seriously look at God's vision for justice, we must take Jesus' return seriously as well.

In His glorious appearing, Jesus will not only come with salvation, but also with vengeance. Today and in the days to come, the Holy Spirit will be emphasizing the face of Jesus as the fierce and righteous Judge. The biblical understanding of Jesus as the

Judge evokes a wide range of emotions, questions, and debates. *Does God judge today? Is hell real? How can a good God bring judgment and send people to eternal torment? Why are His judgments so severe?* These questions and many others drive the discussion on this perplexing and glorious topic.

To understand Jesus' judgments, we must first understand His character and His purpose for the earth. God's vision is to fill this world with His justice through the knowledge of Jesus. The centerpiece of God's eternal purpose is for Jesus to come back to fully establish His kingdom rule over all the earth as He joins the heavenly and earthly realms together (see Eph. 1:9-10).

This plan will not be executed without a battle that is fought on two fronts: spiritual and natural (see Ps. 24:7-10; Isa. 34; Isa. 63; Joel 3; Zeph. 2-3). Commonly the subject of warfare is limited to a battle fought in the spirit. However, there is a battle to be fought at the end of natural history. Though Jesus did not raise up a physical army—and neither will His servants before He returns—during His Second Coming Jesus will come as a warrior king who will wage war with divinely anointed and spiritual arsenal (see Zech. 12:3, 8-9; 14:2-5, 12-15; Rev. 8-9; Rev. 15-16).

The spiritual front was fought on the cross during the First Coming of Jesus, when He disarmed powers and principalities through His death, burial, and resurrection (see Col. 2:15). The Servant of the Lord, Jesus, came to defeat Satan at the cross, to make a public spectacle of powers and principalities, and render realms of darkness powerless now. The purpose of the First Coming and the work of the cross were to lay a foundation upon which Jesus' kingdom will be established forever. In order to build His kingdom, He would first reconcile to Himself the people who would through faith say yes to His leadership and become citizens of His heavenly kingdom which is to come. He delivered them from the bondage of sin and wrote His law, His value system, upon their hearts.

The natural battlefront will be fought at Jesus' return when the kings of the earth under the leadership of the antichrist seek to make war with Him. Jesus will defeat them by releasing the severe end-time judgments of God on the nations (see Isa. 42:13; Ezek. 14:21; Rev. 17:14). This is related to the administration of the Father's vision to bring heaven and earth together, with the goal of manifesting the fullness of His justice in all of society. Jesus, the God-Man who is a warrior, will wage the war for justice by the sword or the rod of His mouth (see Isa. 11; Eph. 6:17; Heb. 4:12; Rev. 1; 19:15), the spoken word in prayer/worship and prophetic decrees.

The Father gave Jesus in His humanity the fullness of the Spirit and the Word by which He would establish justice in the earth (see Isa. 59:21). Justice will go forth through the power of the Spirit in response to the Word of God. The Spirit of God moves when there is agreement with the word of God. Jesus is the embodiment of that full agreement as the Servant of the Lord. As fully God and fully man He agrees with, then prays, proclaims, and practices the Father's decrees in full obedience. Jesus is the ultimate embodiment of this truth and it is the manner in which He will wage war for justice.

The war that Jesus will wage is most commonly referred to by the location in which it takes place: Armageddon (see Rev. 16:16). When most people hear the term "Armageddon", they think of two world powers colliding in a large-scale war, bringing the earth to the brink of destruction. Yet this is not how the Bible describes it. Armageddon is when the kings of the earth will seek to wage war against Jesus (see Rev. 17:14) as He returns to receive the nations as His inheritance (see Ps. 2:8-9) and to establish God's justice in the world. David says that Jesus will effortlessly break the nations, as easily as a man could use an iron rod to smash clay vessels:

> *Ask of Me, and I will give You the nations for Your inheritance, and the ends of the earth for Your possession. You*

shall break them with a rod of iron; You shall dash them to pieces like a potter's vessel (Ps. 2:8-9).

During the battle of Armageddon Jesus will slay the nations with the word of His mouth. He will speak the word and mountains will split; plagues and pestilences will be released; 100 pound hailstones, earthquakes, confusion, madness, blindness, bloodshed, flooding, fire, and brimstone will occur (see Ezek. 38:22; Zech. 14:12-13).

Scripture shows us that Christ will return, not only with salvation, but with a fierceness of judgment to confront and execute evil kings, oppressive regimes, and governments in the earth (see Ps. 110:5-6; Ps. 149:7-9). This is very troubling and offensive to the finite, carnal mind; yet the Word of God clearly shows that this is necessary to accomplish His purpose. The biblical understanding of Jesus as a man of war and righteous Judge gives us insight into the beauty of His nature and informs us of His serious intent to release justice. In fact, the first time God's beauty is referenced it is in the context of Him defeating the armies of Pharaoh's oppressive regime.

The Lord is a man of war; The Lord is His name. Pharaoh's chariots and his army He has cast into the sea; His chosen captains also are drowned in the Red Sea. The depths have covered them; They sank to the bottom like a stone. "Your right hand, O Lord, has become glorious in power; Your right hand, O Lord, has dashed the enemy in pieces. And in the greatness of Your excellence You have overthrown those who rose against You; You sent forth Your wrath; It consumed them like stubble. And with the blast of Your nostrils The waters were gathered together; The floods stood upright like a heap; The depths congealed in the heart of the sea. The enemy said, 'I will pursue, I will overtake, I will divide the spoil; My desire shall be satisfied on them. I will draw my sword, My hand shall

destroy them.' You blew with Your wind, The sea covered
them; They sank like lead in the mighty waters. "Who
is like You, O Lord, among the gods? Who is like You,
glorious in holiness, Fearful in praises, doing wonders?
(Exodus 15:3-11)

Moses declares to us that one of God's divine attributes is "warrior." A divine attribute makes known to us that which is true about the character of God. A.W. Tozer defines an attribute as "a mental concept, an intellectual response to God's self-revelation."[150] God's attributes may seem paradoxical, yet we must realize that God does not suspend one attribute to exercise another. When He releases His judgments, He has not ceased to be the God of mercy. When He reveals Himself as a Warrior, He does not cease to be a Savior.

The Lord desires for us to know both the day of vengeance that is in His heart (see Isa. 63:4), as well as the day of salvation. Paul urged the church in Rome to know the kindness and the severity of the Lord (see Rom. 11:22). It is necessary for us to understand both dynamics, and to observe how He judges and saves, without contradiction in His Person. When we prayerfully consider His holy nature, we will see over time that, rather than standing in conflict to His goodness, the judgments of God magnify how good He really is and how committed He is to justice and love.

As an example, one of the things Jesus will be fighting for at His return is the cause of the orphan (see Ps. 68:5). Even today, we see that children are among the hardest hit by injustice. Children comprise 40-50 percent of the number of people subjected to slavery.[151] In addition to the horrors of sex trafficking, they are bought and sold in various nations as payment for debt, put to long hours of forced labor, and compelled to serve in militias as armed soldiers.[152] Joel prophesied of a time when children will be sold in exchange for prostitution or for alcohol (see Joel 3:3).[153]

Revelation 18 speaks of Babylon being instrumental in selling the bodies and souls of human beings (see Rev. 18:11-13).

During His first coming, Jesus declared that for those who cause His little ones to stumble, it would be better for them to be drowned in the sea with a millstone tied around their neck (see Matt. 18:6; Mark 9:42; Luke 17:2). At the end of the age, we see an angel doing just that.

> *Then a mighty angel took up a stone like a great millstone and threw it into the sea, saying, "Thus with violence the great city Babylon shall be thrown down, and shall not be found anymore. The sound of harpists, musicians, flutists, and trumpeters shall not be heard in you anymore. No craftsman of any craft shall be found in you anymore, and the sound of a millstone shall not be heard in you anymore. The light of a lamp shall not shine in you anymore, and the voice of bridegroom and bride shall not be heard in you anymore. For your merchants were the great men of the earth, for by your sorcery all the nations were deceived. And in her was found the blood of prophets and saints, and of all who were slain on the earth"* (Rev. 18:21-24).

Jesus' anger is stirred on behalf of the orphan. He will shout like a Man of war, He will break in with power and He will tread the nations like the one who treads the winepress.[154] Jesus is zealous to make the wrong things right. He is committed to end all expressions of sin. At the end of the age, there will be a steady decline of morality on all levels—personally, societally, nationally, and globally. The justice of Jesus demands that He bring vengeance upon all these areas. Isaiah says that Jesus comes clothed with salvation and vengeance for justice:

> *For He put on righteousness as a breastplate, And a helmet of salvation on His head; He put on the garments of*

vengeance for clothing, And was clad with zeal as a cloak (Isa. 59:17).

Jesus' clothing in this verse shows that He is fully equipped to bring forth justice among the nations.[155] Here, we can see His glory and beauty as a Man of War. He is the One who both delivers the oppressed and judges the oppressor. God is not passive when it comes to justice. As the poor of the earth ask the question, "Does God even care?" the answer is a resounding "Yes!" (see Isa. 42:13). He loves righteousness and hates wickedness. He will avenge the oppressed that call on His name, and will loose His wrath on anything that stands in the way of His perfect vision for justice on the earth.

The attribute of Jesus as a Man of war is not one that is only seen at Armageddon, because the attributes of God reveal who He is forever. While it is not difficult to imagine the Lord being good, kind, and gentle for all of eternity, it can be difficult to understand that He will be a Man of war forever. To comprehend this, we must also understand Him through His eternal judgments—specifically, the Lake of Fire. The battle of Armageddon and the Lake of Fire are two sides of the same coin.

The battle of Armageddon culminates with Jesus casting the antichrist and the false prophet into the Lake of Fire (see Rev. 19:11-21). Armageddon is the place that Jesus defeats the rebellious kings of the earth, and the Lake of Fire is the place where He will war against all the enemies of love and justice forever, even as they persist forever in their rebellious attitudes against God. Jesus, the Man of War, is seen in both realities.

There is much confusion about the subject of eternal punishment today. This confusion arises when we try to reconcile God's judgments with our own definition of love. At the very core, we are very limited in our understanding of God's goodness and love. Even our highest ideas of God's goodness fall profoundly short of how good He really is. His love is holy—it is transcendent, completely above anything that we could imagine. His goodness is beyond understanding. If we want to grapple with the issue of eternal punishment, we must first grapple with how God's transcendence permeates His attributes of love and goodness.

Aside from the Holy Spirit explaining this to our hearts and our minds, His goodness and His love are beyond our comprehension. Anything that opposes His love is therefore far worse than we can possibly imagine. His infinite, holy love means that anything at enmity with His love is by definition wicked in its scope, and must be dealt with in an eternal way. From this perspective, God's love is not in conflict with the Lake of Fire. His love and His justice necessitate it.

The issue of eternal punishment is not a reflection of a lack of love on God's part. Paul writes that God's love was demonstrated towards us in that, while we were yet His enemies, He sent His Son to die for us (see Rom. 5:6-8). The debt of humanity was so severe that only God Himself in the flesh could pay it. He did not have to pay our debt, but in His mercy and goodness towards us, He did pay it. We truly cannot comprehend the weight of this truth. Eternal punishment comes when humans stubbornly refuse the precious gift of a King—His own darling Son who became flesh. Those who refuse to be covered by the payment Jesus made will have to pay off their own debt to God in the Lake of Fire—and because the debt is infinite, their punishment is eternal.

Jesus' love and justice are a consistent reflection of His nature. As much as the God of love desires to reconcile all people to Himself, He is also fiercely opposed to the evil that will hinder and resist that love. Jesus' love is inseparable from His righteousness and truth, and He will not compromise these attributes under a false pretense of peace. The understanding of Jesus as a fierce and righteous Judge will give the church, the poor, and the oppressed of the earth assurance that justice will come to those who entrust their lives under the leadership of Jesus (see Isa. 9:7;

42:13; 2 Thess. 1:6-8). In His love and goodness, He will ultimately and eternally deal with every wrong thing on this earth. Because Jesus is a loving and zealous Man of war, we have assurance that the justice God desires will prevail for all of eternity.

Chapter 10

Already, But Not Yet

The apostles who followed Jesus were bold in their proclamation that salvation was found in no other name than the name of Jesus (see Acts 4:12). Jesus Christ is the only hope for true and lasting social justice in the earth. As the Redeemer of society and Savior of mankind, the salvation that Jesus brings is holistic. Jesus came to take away sin and cleanse its individual and societal effects on the world. When He was born, this caused the angels to break forth in exultant praise. They trumpeted Jesus' intended purpose for all of created order: *"Glory to God in the highest, And on earth peace, goodwill toward men!"* (Luke 2:14).

Jesus' ultimate mission in coming to the earth is to fill every sphere of society with shalom and destroy everything that stands in its way (see 1 John 3:8). The whole earth will be consumed with the radiant fire of His glory, experiencing the fullness of His righteousness and justice when He establishes His government on the earth (see Hab. 2:14; Luke 12:49). This is our sure hope for the future.

The reality we face today, however, is that injustice is deeply impacting the whole earth. The issues can seem insurmountable. Every sphere of life is rife with injustice: adultery, divorce, and child abuse destroy our families; our governments propagate unjust wars and immigration laws; abortion and human trafficking plague our societies. It would be difficult to list every way in which injustice touches our lives, our environments, and our cultures.

Worldwide, 100 million homeless children live in the streets, and 250,000 children die every week from disease and malnutrition.[156] Nearly 900 million people live in hunger worldwide.[157] According to the United Nations, it would cost $30 billion to solve this issue of world hunger[158]—yet America alone spends $134 billion dollars per year on fast food,[159] and just in 2007, global military expenditure was a staggering $1.3 trillion.[160]

It is difficult to consider the overwhelming magnitude of this sort of injustice. Some people grow bitter and jaded in the face of this seemingly endless stream of injustice. Others simply tune out, deciding that this is just the way things are, and that nothing really can be done on this side of eternity.

Yet Jesus is not indifferent about these issues. He feels pain concerning the injustices that are running rampant in the earth. For this reason, He came to establish salvation through His cross. Though salvation will be fully manifest when Jesus returns and sets up His government in Jerusalem, He can, and does, break in with justice today, making wrong things right. He wants His people to participate with Him in His purposes. As we contend for justice today through intercession and the proclamation of the gospel with power and good deeds, there is a partial, but significant, manifestation of justice that can be released.

Not only are real measures of justice possible in this age, believers around the world have already seen it taking place. Historically, we can point to the Second Great Awakening and the Welsh Revival. Today, we can point to Almolonga, Guatemala, and the nation of Fiji as two key examples of the gospel bringing about social change.

Historical: The Second Great Awakening

In the United States, a revival broke out in the 1790s which continued through the 1850s. This became known as the Second Great Awakening, and was marked by an unprecedented increase of church attendance and religious zeal. Many social reform movements were birthed out of this awakening, including women's suffrage, abolitionism, and temperance societies. Participants shared the belief that social action could be effected by individuals, and that it was part of God's plan. This awakening was committed to both personal and societal reform.

Charles Finney, a notable leader in the revival, proclaimed that slavery was a national sin. The gospel he preached gave anti-slavery activists a theological foundation to pursue immediate emancipation. This urgency prompted abolitionists to cast off their previous approaches of gradual abolition.[161]

Historical: 1904 Welsh Revival

In 1904, a revival broke out in Wales that would eventually sweep across the globe. Believers in Loughor, South Wales had been praying for God to come and meet them and touch their nation, when one night the power of the Holy Spirit suddenly fell upon the group with conviction. Word got out quickly to neighboring towns and villages, and many people repented of their sin. The revival spread like wildfire, and soon all of Wales felt the effects.

Throughout the revival, scores of people gathered in nightly meetings,[162] which were marked by prayer and singing, often lasting several hours.[163] Within a very short time, the social impact of the Welsh revival was widely evident. After only a month of meetings, many bars and taverns closed as people gave up drinking and gambling. Coal mines temporarily shut down when the work ponies stopped responding to the miners' commands, no longer recognizing them due to the sudden lack of curse words.[164] During one six-month period of the revival, one hundred thousand people gave their lives to Jesus.[165]

The weighty presence of God was felt throughout Wales. From churches and chapels to homes, businesses, bars, and train stations, God's Spirit was manifest.[166] The Welsh Revival transformed the culture, changing the way people did business, interacted with one another, and behaved in the community. The justice of Jesus' kingdom was seen in the present day.

Today: Almolonga, Guatemala

Before the 1970s, the residents of Almolonga, Guatemala, were steeped in occult practices and idol worship. The rampant use of alcohol led to violence and poverty throughout the city. Family structures were broken and dysfunctional. Local jails were at times filled to overflowing.

In the mid-1970s, a group of believers in Almolonga began praying together on a regular basis. As they cried out to God, they began to see evidence that He was changing the culture of their city. Many men and women were delivered from demons. A prominent priest of witchcraft, along with his family, repented and turned to Christ, burning idols and witchcraft paraphernalia. Many people were also supernaturally healed. Today, 65 percent of Almolonga's residents follow Jesus.[167] The church continues to fast and pray, believing for God to do in other cities what He has done in theirs.[168] Almolonga is a testimony to Jesus' ability to change an entire city from the inside out.

Today: The Nation of Fiji

For most of its history, the islands of Fiji were filled with a culture of witchcraft and idolatry. Under such spiritual darkness, the land suffered, producing a vicious cycle of poverty, unrest, foul water, and poor agricultural yields.

Yet in the 21st century, revival began sweeping through Fiji. Spurred on by this, believers in the village of Nataleira—a place which suffered many environmental hardships—began to cry out to Jesus for the healing of their land. They met for a solemn assembly, praying from nine o'clock in the morning until midnight for two weeks. God heard their cries and answered them in very visible, profound ways. A certain type of fish that had reportedly not been seen for many years returned to the village, boosting the economy and local food supply.

In the village of Nuku, believers sought God in fasting and prayer, renouncing their agreement with idolatry. A stream that had been toxic for over forty years was miraculously made clean. Other villages began turning to the Lord for healing and saw the same kinds of miracles. Coral reefs came back to life, shellfish populations increased, and fruit grew larger and more abundantly than ever before. This pattern of repentance, fasting, and prayer, followed by the divine healing of the environment, continued throughout many parts of Fiji. Eventually it spread even into neighboring nations.[169]

The Lord gave a conditional promise to His people in 2 Chronicles 7:14 that, if they repented of their wickedness and prayed, He would answer their cry and heal their land. The island nation of Fiji is a modern-day fulfillment of this promise, showing how this kind of justice can take place even in this age.

Jesus, Anointed for Justice

Jesus is the only Man able to establish the justice that God desires in the nations of the earth. Every attempt of secular leaders to establish justice throughout history has either failed or fallen short. For example, slaves in Haiti sought freedom, only to give birth to the poorest nation in the Western Hemisphere.[170] Che Guevara hated the violence of capitalism, but his efforts to effect social change simply perpetuated a cycle of violence. Mere human efforts are not enough.

In Isaiah 42:1, Isaiah declared that the Father has put His Spirit upon His divine Son, the Servant. Jesus was given supernatural endowment to establish and administrate justice. For this reason we can trust that Jesus will bring about true and lasting justice on the earth—He will not fail (see Isa. 42:4).

Jesus possesses all power, wisdom, and insight by the Holy Spirit to establish the government of His Father in every facet of society. Isaiah 11 is a key passage which highlights the seven-fold manifestation of the Holy Spirit on the Messiah who is empowered by the Spirit to establish justice in the earth:

> The Spirit of the Lord shall rest upon Him, The Spirit of wisdom and understanding, The Spirit of counsel and might, The Spirit of knowledge and of the fear of the Lord (Isa. 11:2).

Isaiah says the Spirit of the Lord will "rest upon" Jesus (see Isa. 11:2). This means that the Messiah is anointed by God and supernaturally enabled to accomplish His plan. The "Spirit of wisdom and understanding" describes Christ's ability to apply the plan of God with insight and to navigate complex issues of individuals and societies. The "Spirit of counsel and might" reveals that Jesus is a military strategist—He will rule the nations with a rod of iron (see Ps. 2:9), and will execute divine judgment even during the millennium (see Zech. 14:17-19), up until the very last war with rebellious nations of the earth (see Rev. 20:7-10). The "Spirit of knowledge and the fear of the Lord" speaks of Jesus' devotional life and intimacy with the Father. He is anointed for intimacy and the fear of the Lord.

In Isaiah 61:1-3, Isaiah further expounds how Jesus establishes justice under the anointing of the Spirit, in measure today and in fullness at His return and eternal kingdom.[171] Jesus quotes this passage in Luke 4:18 to declare the mission of His First Coming, as well as to reveal His identity as the Messiah who brings about ultimate justice in the age to come:

> *The Spirit of the Lord God is upon Me, because the Lord has anointed Me To preach good tidings to the poor; He has sent Me To heal the brokenhearted, To proclaim liberty to the captives, and the opening of the prison to those who are bound; To proclaim the acceptable year of the Lord, and the day of vengeance of our God; To comfort all who mourn, To console those who mourn in Zion, To give them beauty for ashes, the oil of joy for mourning, the garment of praise for the spirit of heaviness; that they may be called trees of righteousness, the planting of the Lord, that He may be glorified* (Isa. 61:1-3).

This operation of the Spirit has continued since the First Coming of Christ, but will be brought to its intended fulfillment when Jesus returns to the earth to establish His government.

The full manifestation of the justice God desires comes forth when Christ establishes His theocratic government on the earth. He will judge the poor, administrate with equity, issue forth divine discipline, try criminals, cleanse the environment, lead the animal kingdom into peace, heal enmity between people and animals, and fill the earth with the fullness of His glory. In other words, Jesus will directly oversee every possible sphere of life. This will take place over a period of a thousand years, known as the Millennium. This is the time period which will transition the whole earth into the full consummation of God's glory and justice for the rest of eternity.

To Preach Good News to the Poor

The gospel is the message of God's plan for justice. It is good news to the poor and the oppressed, because even as it includes transformation of the depravity of their hearts, it is the message of the complete and glorious justice which God will bring to the earth.

It gives them dignity and the hope to become first-class citizens—even kings—in Jesus' coming kingdom through the born-again experience.[172] The gospel is the good news to the poor and the oppressed because it gives assurance of God's will coming to pass. It is a message of future hope, with profound bearing on their lives today, that can sustain the poor in the midst of their plight.

Jesus shares this anointing for good news with His church. The people of God will partner with Jesus as messengers of His soon-coming righteous society on the earth. As the deception of the false justice movement increases, God will increase the empowerment of His Spirit upon the church to declare the truth of His desire to transform both individuals and societies. The people of God will be anointed with a message of hope—both for this age and the next—that is far superior to anything offered by the false justice movement.

To Heal the Brokenhearted

The evil of injustice has caused untold trauma to the human race. Divorce has left broken individuals and families in its wake.[173] Bullying in school systems amongst teenagers has precipitated teen suicide and school shooting rampages.[174] People of all ages and many nationalities have been wounded by racial discrimination and hatred. Untold numbers of individuals and people groups have suffered under the effects of sin, demonic oppression, and societal injustice. Yet Jesus will intimately attend to and heal the hearts of His people.

In Jesus' coming kingdom, He will bring full healing to these injustices, stopping their influence forever (see Isa. 35:10, 51:11; Rev 21:4). Yet even now, Christ and His gospel can address and bring healing and restoration to these issues. When we follow Christ, He deals with sin by healing the effects of the sin we've committed, as well the sin others have committed against us. This happens primarily by the Spirit, the life of Christ, taking residence in the hearts of those who say yes to Christ and His leadership (see Col. 1:27; 2:9-10).

To Proclaim Liberty to the Captives, and the Opening of the Prison to Those Who Are Bound

Jesus has the authority to deliver those held captive and oppressed by spiritual and social forces. He will deliver not only those oppressed by demons, but also those suffering unjust imprisonment, including slaves, women trapped in brothels, and victims of human trafficking (see Isa. 49:8-9; Acts 12:1, 5-7; Acts 16:26). In the New Testament, we see Jesus setting free those held captive by both demonic powers and physical prisons (see Matt. 8:28-32; Acts 10:38).

When Peter was imprisoned by Herod for his faith in Christ, the prayers of the church accomplished his miraculous release:

> *Peter was therefore kept in prison, but constant prayer was offered to God for him by the church...that night Peter was sleeping, bound with two chains between two soldiers; and the guards before the door were keeping the prison. Now behold, an angel of the Lord stood by him, and a light shone in the prison; and he struck Peter on the side and raised him up, saying, "Arise quickly!" And his chains fell off his hands* (Acts 12:5-7).

Today, Jesus is still setting free both spiritual and natural captives. One stunning example of this is Brother Yun, a Chinese Christian who was imprisoned multiple times for preaching the gospel. During one prison sentence, the prison guards beat him so severely that he was left with crushed bones in his legs, relying completely on other prisoners to carry him from place to place. But suddenly, on the morning of May 5, 1997, the Holy Spirit spoke to him, telling him, "Go now! The God of Peter is your God." Yun rose to his feet—instantly healed—and through a series of supernaturally influenced events, from open gates to blinded guards, he simply walked out of the high-security prison that held him.[175]

To Proclaim the Acceptable Year of the Lord, and the Day of Vengeance of Our God

Church history since the cross of Christ—when Jesus canceled our debts by His propitiatory death—can be said to be the year of the Lord's favor (see Col. 2:13-14). The acceptable year of the Lord is a window of mercy which reveals Jesus' forgiveness and redemption. But we are swiftly approaching the day of His vengeance when God will release end-time judgments on the earth right before His Son returns. The justice of God requires both salvation and vengeance—salvation for the oppressed who call on Jesus' name, and vengeance upon the people and institutions which oppose His leadership. We do not choose between the two aspects—Jesus is anointing the church to proclaim both.

To Console Those Who Mourn; To Comfort All Who Mourn in Zion

The Holy Spirit comforts those who have repented of their sins as they mourn over them. He will also console those who are mourning due to the trauma of societal sin inflicted upon them. The Spirit alone can heal and comfort all who mourn, from those who have committed the sin of abortion, to the women, girls and boys suffering in Eastern European brothels. People groups who have a long-standing history of oppression need the power of the Holy Spirit in order to find the restoration of their dignity and purpose. Jesus will heal the hearts of individuals and entire people groups when He returns, and He moves with emotional restoration even today.

In addition to healing His peoples' hearts, Jesus is also a healer of physical infirmity. One of the greatest tragedies that came as a result of the fall of Adam was that the human race became susceptible to sickness and disease. Every human being is impacted in some way by sickness. Studies show that in 2005, 133 million Americans were dealing with some kind of chronic physical problem; that number is expected to double by 2020. Americans spend $850 billion annually on pharmaceuticals.[176] Approximately 14.8 million children in sub-Saharan Africa are orphaned due to the AIDS crisis, often ostracized by society, abandoned by family, and forced to beg for basic necessities of life.[177] At various times through history, disease has threatened to wipe out entire civilizations.[178] The social and financial implications of this sort of oppression are vast. Sickness is an injustice that robs humanity of finances, relationships, dignity, and purpose (see John 10:10).

Beauty, Joy, and Praise

In light of this kind of suffering, we need a flood of the Spirit's healing power to be released upon the nations of the earth. And this is what the Spirit is calling upon the Lord Jesus to do—bring consolation to the mourning and broken. When people are healed, their body is made whole, and the significance of that cannot be minimized. But God also redeems the ash heap sickness made of their lives, giving them beauty for ashes. Physical healing brings restoration of the body and the soul, as the Spirit gives the oil of joy for mourning.

Victims of injustice, regardless of whether it stems from sickness, personal sins, or societal oppression, are often plagued with depression and all kinds of emotional trauma. But the justice Jesus brings through healing and deliverance establishes a spirit of worship, the garment of praise. The great result of all this is that those delivered and healed by Christ will become strong oaks of righteousness to the glory of God. They become trophies of the grace of God, to the praise of the glory of His grace.

Jesus, the Anointed One, is able to bring true, deep, and lasting justice. His Gospel truly is good news to the poor. Both in this age and in the age to come, He will not fail in bringing forth the justice that God desires.

Where Do We Go from Here?

In the Olivet Discourse (see Matt. 24-25), Jesus gave a very clear exhortation about how we are to live, particularly as it pertains to the generation of His return. He told His disciples various things that will take place in an intensified manner in that generation. He spoke of wars, famines, and diseases. He spoke of false prophets and martyrdom and betrayal (see Matt. 24:5-7). And in the midst of it all, of all the advice that Jesus could give to His people, He called them to watch and pray (see Matt. 24:42; 25:13).

Undoubtedly, there are other things that the church will do to get ready for the challenges present at the end of the age. However, the thing that Jesus insisted upon is that His people would pray. It is for this reason that the Holy Spirit is raising up a night and day prayer movement in the world (see Isa. 62:6).

In addition, Jesus states in Matthew 24:14 that this gospel of the kingdom will be preached in all the nations and then the end will come. The message of God's justice through Christ Jesus will be proclaimed with power, signs, and wonders. We must give ourselves to communicating the gospel, which has two components: preaching and practice. Preaching involves the verbal communication of the truth of Jesus and His plan. Practice is the doing of good deeds—deeds of compassion, service, and justice. We must "Preach the gospel and if necessary use words."[179] There is an action element to the gospel as well as a verbal component.

Jesus began His exhortation with a warning about deception (see Matt. 24:4), and when He highlighted this, He did so while underlining the various troubles that will touch the nations in the last days, such as civil war, global wars, natural disasters, hunger, and disease. The reason Jesus is warning against deception is because it will hinder the church from fully obeying the exhortation to pray and proclaim God's glorious plan for justice—a justice that was purchased on the cross and will fully manifest when Jesus returns. This plan is the gospel.

The global nature of these crises will create a context where the cry for justice grows, which will give rise to false messengers. Jesus goes on to warn against lawlessness. Many of the agents of counterfeit justice have undermined the governments under which they lived. True messengers will call for the submission to government—oppressive regimes—to not resist them but rather wait on the Lord in prayer while announcing the gospel of Jesus Christ (see Matt. 23:1-3; 26:52; Rom. 13:1-2; 1 Pet. 2:13-17).

The false ideologies that false messengers espouse will be powerless to drive the human soul to seek Jesus. Instead of prayer and the message of true faith, these false messengers will move hearts to take matters into their own hands. Herein lies the deception that can undermine the end-time prayer movement.

There is a seeming weakness in embracing prayer and speaking the truth of the cross of Christ. The human tendency is to take on justice in our own strength and be moved by our own sense of right and wrong. False teaching ultimately drives us to put our trust in our self. The gospel and prayer call us to a place of utter dependence on the Lord. These will be the premier weapons of the end-time church to combat injustice.

In light of all of this, we must prepare ourselves through various ways. At the International House of Prayer of Kansas City Missions Base, we have what we call the sacred charge. The sacred charge consists of seven practical commitments to begin walking out a lifestyle of preparation:

* *Pray Daily:* connecting with God while changing the world by releasing His power;

* *Fast Weekly:* positioning ourselves to receive more from God by fasting two days a week;

* *Do Justly:* being zealous for good works of compassion and justice that exalt Jesus as we impact the seven spheres of society;

* *Give Extravagantly:* experiencing the joy of financial power encounters as we sacrificially give money to the kingdom and support the prayer movement;

* *Live Holy:* living fascinated in the pleasure of loving God that overflows to loving people;

* *Lead Diligently:* taking the initiative to minister to others and make disciples by regularly leading in outreaches, prayer meetings, and Bible studies;

* *Speak Boldly:* being a faithful witness of the truth with allegiance to Jesus' Word.[180]

The experience of entertaining the thought of abortion while in prayer before the Lord left an indelible mark on me. I was reminded that I too was a man in need of grace and mercy. Beloved, in our "unrenewed man" there is a human trafficker; in all of us there is a murderer (see Jer. 17:9; Matt. 15:18-19). However, when we come into Jesus' presence, we can unveil our hearts before Him to find mercy and grace, and let Him wash us with His presence and His power. It is amazing how, after we have been found guilty, He forgives us, gives us mercy, and then launches us like an arrow to be His messengers against the very thing that we partook of. This is good news!

Micah tells us that we are required to pursue justice with tenderness and humility. Essential to this process is the understanding that justice starts with our own need to be justified. *"For God so loved the world that He gave His only begotten Son..."* (see John 3:16). When one stops to think on this verse, it helps us see this truth. The world that Jesus is referring to is the world that is filled with darkness, a place that is filled with racism, oppression, human trafficking, abortion, hunger, genocide, kidnapping, wars, government corruption (see 1 Tim. 1:8-11).

God, though angry and displeased with the world (see Ps. 7:11; Isa. 59:16), deeply loves the abortion doctor, the human trafficker and the racist, as well as their victims, and He gave His Son to die on the cross for them. God is in the business of converting human traffickers and making them into bestselling songwriters like John Newton, the author of "Amazing Grace." Some of the premier songwriters in the end-time worship movement may have testimonies like this former slave trader.

When we pray for the ending of injustice, let us take a stand not only for the oppressed but for the oppressor as well. It is important that as we move forward in taking a stand for justice that we do it in a way prescribed by God. We must pursue justice tenderly and walk humbly with God in intimacy. It is what God requires.

NOTES

1. Ludwig Koehler and Walter Baumgartner, *The Hebrew and Aramaic Lexicon Of The Old Testament IV*, trans., ed. M.E.J. Richardson (Boston: Brill, 1999), 1506-1510.

2. A list of 150 chapters on the end times can be found at www.mikebickle.org/resources/resource/2888.

3. Michael D. Palmer and Stanley M. Burgess, eds., *The Wiley-Blackwell Companion to Religion and Social Justice* (West Sussex: Blackwell Publishing Limited, 2012), 137.

4. *Islam: Empire of Faith*, DVD. Produced by Robert Gardner. PBS, 2000.

5. Ibid.

6. Karen Armstrong, *Muhammad. A Biography of the Prophet* (New York: HarperCollins Publishers, 1992), 45.

7. Ibid., 91.

8. Ibid., 93.

9. Karen Armstrong, *Buddha* (New York: Penguin Putnam Inc., 2001), 1-3.

10. Ibid., 62-63, 71.

11. Ibid., 81-83.

12. Markus Bockmuehl and James Carleton Paget, ed., *Redemption and Resistance: The Messianic Hopes of Jews and Christians in Antiquity* (New York: T&T Clark, 2007), 40.

13. James J. Bloom, *The Jewish Revolts Against Rome, A.D. 66-135: A Military Analysis* (Jefferson: McFarland & Company, Inc., 2010), 202-203.

14. Ibid., 210.

15. Julius Hillel Greenstone, *The Messiah Idea in Jewish History* (Philadelphia: The Jewish Publication Society of America, 1906), 89-90.

16. Bloom, *Jewish Revolts*, 205.

17. Ibid., 206.

18. Ibid., 208.

19. Francis Wheen, *Karl Marx: A Life* (New York: W.W. Norton & Company, 2000), 10.

20. Ann M. Woodall, *What Price the Poor?: William Booth, Karl Marx and the London Residuum* (Aldershot: Ashgate Publishing Limited, 2005), 88-89.

21. Ibid., 112-113.

22. Hans Schwarz, *Eschatology* (Grand Rapids: Wm. B. Eerdmans Publishing Company, 2000), 219.

23. Max I. Dimont, *Jews, God and History* (New York: New American Library, 1994), 347.

24. William David Davies, *Christian Engagements with Judaism* (Harrisburg: Trinity Press International, 1999), 11.

25. Wheen, *Karl Marx*, 1.

26. Richard L. Harris, *Che Guevara: A Biography* (Santa Barbara: Greenwood, 2011), 194-196.

27. *The True Story of Che Guevara*, DVD. Produced by Maria Berry. History Channel, 2007.

28. Ernesto "Che" Guevara, *The Motorcycle Diaries*, (New York: Ocean Press, 2004), 167-168.

29. *The True Story of Che Guevara*, DVD. Produced by Maria Berry. History Channel, 2007.

30. Jorge G. Castañeda, *Compañero: The Life and Death of Che Guevara* (New York: Vintage Books, 1997), 83.

31. Jon Lee Anderson, *Che Guevara: A Revolutionary Life* (New York: Grove Press, 1997), 387.

32. Ibid., 726.

33. Ibid., 730.

34. Ibid.

35. Catherine Wessinger, *How the Millennium Comes Violently: From Jonestown to Heaven's Gate* (New York: Seven Bridges Press, 2000), 32.

36. Ibid.

37. Wessinger, *Millennium*, 34.

38. William M. Ashcraft and Eugene V. Gallagher, ed., *Introduction to New and Alternative Religions in America* (Westport: Greenwood Press, 2006), 117.

39. David Chidester, *Salvation and Suicide: An Interpretation of Jim Jones, the Peoples Temple, and Jonestown* (Bloomington: Indiana University Press, 2003), 56-57.

40. Ibid., 60.

41. John MacArthur, *Matthew 1-7, Volume 1* (Chicago: Moody Bible Institute, 1985), 463.

42. Brian Haughton, *Hidden History: Lost Civilizations, Secret Knowledge, and Ancient Mysteries* (Franklin Lakes: Career Press, 2007), 51-53; Andrew Lang, *Tales of Troy and Greece* (New York: Longmans, Green, and Co., 1907), 101-110; Barry Strauss, *The Trojan War: A New History* (New York: Simon and Schuster, 2006), 171-179.

43. Abbe A. Debolt and James S. Baugess, *Encyclopedia of the Sixties: A Decade of Culture and Counterculture* (Santa Barbara: Greenwood, 2012), 127.

44. See, for instance, Warren Buffet and Bill Gates and their "Giving Pledge"; Angelina Jolie's appointment as the ambassador of goodwill to the United Nations High Commissioner of Refugees; George Clooney and his advocacy for Sudan; Hugh Jackman's work with the Global Poverty Project; Bono's efforts

regarding global hunger; and the Tim Tebow Foundation; just to name a few.

45. Guler Aras and David Crowther, eds., *NGOs and Social Responsibility* (Bingley: Emerald Group Publishing Limited, 2010), 114; Paul Hawken, *Blessed Unrest: How the Largest Social Movement in History Is Restoring Grace, Justice, and Beauty to the World* (New York: Viking Penguin, 2007), 2; "Quick Facts About Nonprofits," National Center for Charitable Statistics (NCCS), accessed April 13, 2012, http://nccs.urban.org/statistics/quickfacts.cfm.

46. Phoebe Hirsch-Dubin, "Web Guide for Social Justice Sites," accessed March 24, 2012, www.education.ucsb.edu/socialjustice/webguide.pdf.

47. Michael Spencer, "The Coming Evangelical Collapse," The Christian Science Monitor, March 10, 2009, accessed April 16, 2009, http://www.csmonitor.com/2009/0310/p09s01-coop.html.

48. William M. Ramsey, *Four Modern Prophets* (Atlanta: John Knox Press, 1986), 10.

49. Janet Forsythe Fishburn, *The Fatherhood of God and the Victorian Family: The Social Gospel in America* (Quebec: McGill-Queen's University Press, 1994), 3-4.

50. Ramsey, *Prophets*, 11.

51. Fishburn, *Fatherhood of God*, 4.

52. Ramsey, *Prophets*, 13.

53. Walter Rauschenbusch, *Christianizing the Social Order* (New York: The MacMillan Co., 1914), 93.

54. Paul M. Minus, *Walter Rauschenbusch: American Reformer* (New York: Macmillan Publishers, 1988), 40.

55. Walter Rauschenbusch, *A Theology for the Social Gospel* (New York: Macmillan Publishers, 1922), 148.

56. Ibid., 243.

57. Ibid., 265.

58. Ibid., 233.

59. When talking about the false justice movement, what is being addressed is the false message that is being proclaimed, not their humanitarian efforts.

60. Brian McLaren, *A New Kind of Christianity* (New York: HarperCollins, 2010), 48.

61. Ibid., 113.

62. Adolf Harnack, *History of Dogma, Volume I*, trans. Neil Buchanan (of 3rd German edition), 273-279, accessed May 8, 2012, http://www.ccel.org/ccel/harnack/dogma1.ii.iii.v.html.

63. Alister McGrath, *Heresy: A History of Defending the Truth*, (New York: HarperCollins, 2009), 128.

64. Ernest Evans, ed., trans., *Tertullian: Adversus Marcionem* (London: Oxford University Press, 1972), x.

65. Ibid., 114.

66. Tony Jones, *Postmodern Youth Ministry* (Grand Rapids: Zondervan, 2001), 201.

67. Tony Jones, *A Better Atonement: Beyond the Depraved Doctrine of Original Sin* (Minneapolis: The JoPa Group, 2012), Kindle edition.

68. Ibid.

69. Ibid.

70. Tony Jones, "Brian McLaren on 'Becoming Convergent,'" emergent-us, August 9, 2005, accessed May 6, 2012, http://emergent-us.typepad.com/emergentus/2005/08/brian_mclaren_o.html.

71. Kathleen E.A. Montheith and Glen Richards, ed., *Jamaica in Slavery and Freedom: History Heritage and Culture* (Kingston: University of the West Indies Press, 2002), 42.

72. Gary Jeffrey, *Bob Marley: The Life of A Musical Legend* (New York: The Rowen Publishing Group, Inc., 2007), 4.

73. Leonard E. Barrett, *The Rastafarians: Sounds of Cultural Dissonance* (Boston: Beacon Press, 1977), 65.

74. Ibid., xii.

75. Ibid., 66.

76. Noel Leo Erskine, *From Garvey to Marley: Rastafari Theology (History of African-American Religions)* (Gainesville: University Press of Florida, 2005), 2.

77. Barrett, *Rastafarians*, 67.

78. Emperor Salassie ruled from 1930-1974

79. Barrett, *Rastafarians*, xxiii.

80. Erskine, *Garvey to Marley*, xv.

81. Ibid., 126.

82. Ibid., 126.

83. Ibid., 48-49.

84. Ibid., 73.

85. Ibid., 68.

86. Ibid., 48.

87. Ibid.

88. Brian McLaren, *A New Kind of Christianity* (New York: HarperCollins, 2010), 215.

89. Some examples of how syncretism is coming together with the social justice movement are: the Coexist Foundation, One Campaign, and "A Common Word Between Us."

90. Jacqueline Ching, *Genocide and The Bosnian War (Genocide in Modern Times),* (New York: Rosen Publishing Group, 2009), 6.

91. Douglas Hamilton Johnson, *The Root Causes of Sudan's Civil Wars* (Bloomington: Indiana University Press, 2003), xv; Lina Sapienza,"Classifying the Killings in Sudan as Genocide," accessed April 7, 2012, http://heinonline.org/HOL/LandingPage?collection=journals&handle=hein.journals/nylshr19&div=55&id=&page.

92. Christine Kinealy, *War and Peace: Ireland since the 1960s* (London: Reaktion Books, 2010), 35-37; "Northern Ireland Conflict: Violence on all sides," accessed April 10, 2012, http://news.bbc.co.uk/2/shared/spl/hi/pop_ups/quick_guides/04/uk_northern_ireland_conflict/html/1.stm.

93. Hassan Fattah, "New Iraqi school spans chasms between religions," *The Christian Science Monitor*, October 7, 2003, accessed July 11, 2011, http://www.csmonitor.com/2003/1007/p01s04-woiq.html.

94. Dietrich Bonhoeffer, *The Cost of Discipleship* (New York: Touchstone, 1995).

95. Jeffrey, *Marley*, 7.

96. Timothy White, *Catch a Fire: The Life of Bob Marley* (New York: St. Martin's Press, 2006), 21.

97. Jason Toynbee, *Bob Marley: Herald of a Postcolonial World?* (Cambridge, UK: Polity Press, 2007), 28.

98. Jeffery, *Marley*, 7.

99. *Marley*. Directed by Kevin MacDonald. Magnolia Pictures, 2012.

100. Hank Bordowitz, *Every Little Thing Gonna Be Alright: The Bob Marley Reader:* (Cambridge: Da Capo Press, 2004), 146.

101. Ibid., 148-150.

102. Ibid., 148-151.

103. Ibid., 201.

104. White, *Catch a Fire*, 21-22.

105. Chris Salewicz, *Bob Marley: The Untold Story* (New York: Faber and Faber Inc., 2009), 367.

106. Zack O'Malley Greenburg, "The Top-Earning Dead Celebrities" *Forbes.com*, October 31, 2011, accessed April 4, 2012, http://www.forbes.com/sites/dorothypomerantz/2011/10/25/the-top-earning-dead-celebrities/.

107. Daniel White Hodge, *The Soul of Hip Hop: Rims, Timbs and a Cultural Theology* (Downers Grove: Intervarsity Press, 2010), 143-144.

108. Josh Nisker. "'Only God Can Judge Me': Tupac Shakur, the Legal System, and Lyrical Subversion." *Journal of Criminal Justice and Popular Culture* 14, no. 1 (2007), 179, http://www.albany.edu/scj/jcjpc/vol14is2/nisker.pdf.

109. Ibid., 180-181.

110. Dipannita Basu and Sidney J. Lemelle, *The Vinyl Ain't Final: Hip Hop and the Globalization of Black Popular Culture* (London: Pluto Press, 2006), 79.

111. Exodus Cry, "Testimonies," May 2008, accessed April 23, 2012, http://exoduscry.com/about/testimonies/.

112. Ibid.

113. Ibid.

114. Robert Kyser, *John, the Maverick Gospel* (Louisville: Westminster John Knox Press, 2007), 54.

115. *Merriam-Webster's Collegiate Dictionary*, 11th ed., (2003), "word".

116. The new song is mentioned nine times in scripture: Ps. 33:3; 40:3; 96:1; 98:1; 144:9; 149:1; Isa. 42:10; Rev. 5:9; 14:3.

117. See Isa. 26:9; 29:24; Jer. 5:4-5; 23:20; 30:24; 31:9, 12-14; Dan. 11:33-35; 12:3, 10; Mal. 4:6; Matt. 17:11; John 14:12; Acts 2:17; Rev. 11:3-6; 18:20. Great Harvest: Dan. 7:14, 27; Matt. 24:14; 28:19; Rev. 5:9; 7:9; 14:6; 15:4. Divine Judgment: Rev. 5:8; 6; 8-9; 15-16.

118. See Isa. 24:14-16; 25:9; 26:8-9; 27:2-5, 13; 30:18-19; 42:10-13; 43:26; 51:11; 52:8; 62:6-7; Jer. 3:17; Joel 2:12-17, 32; Mic. 5:3-4; Zeph. 2:1-3; Zech. 13:9d; Matt. 21:13; Luke 18:7-8; Rev. 5:8; 8:3-5; 22:17, 20.

119. For more information see www.thecall.com.

120. For more information see www.nationaldayofprayer.org.

121. Tom Hess, "Rise of the Praying Church," *Charisma Magazine*, May 1, 2011, accessed April 11, 2012, http://charismamag.com/index.php/features/30830-rise-of-the-praying-church.

122. For more information see www.tzhop.co.nz.

123. Rick Rupp, Director of Topeka House of Prayer and Intercessory Missionary at IHOP-KC, April 11, 2012.

124. Hess, "Rise of the Praying Church."

125. Ibid.

126. For more information see www.anticipando.org.

127. For more information see www.24-7prayer.com.

128. Hess, "Rise of the Praying Church."

129. For more information see www.ihop-atlanta.com.

130. For more information see www.Luke18project.com.

131. Adrienne S. Gaines, "Ministry Seeks to Plant Houses of Prayer at Every U.S. College," Charisma Magazine, December 24, 2009, accessed April 10, 2012, http://www.charismamag.com/index.php/news-old/25764-ministry-seeks-to-plant-house-of-prayer-at-every-us-college-campuses.

132. Melissa del Bosque "The Deadliest Place in Mexico: Who's killing the people of the Juarez Valley?" accessed April 12, 2012, http://www.texasobserver.org/cover-story/the-deadliest-place-in-mexico; "Mexico drug wars: Murders down in Ciudad Juarez," accessed April 12, 2012, http://www.bbc.co.uk/news/world-latin-america-17082002.

133. Sada Rogers, Intercessory Missionary at IHOP-KC, April 11, 2012.

134. Olga R. Rodriguez, "Mexico's largest pot bust likely hit Sinaloa gang," accessed April 12, 2012, http://www.utsandiego.com/news/2010/oct/19/mexicos-largest-pot-bust-likely-hit-sinaloa-gang/.

135. "May 2010," Exodus Cry, accessed February 17, 2012, http://exoduscry.com/about/testimonies; William Sherman, "Bloods

gang members went to Brooklyn schools to recruit under-
age girls as hookers: prosecutors," Daily News, June 2, 2010,
accessed March 7, 2012, http://www.nydailynews.com/news/
crime/bloods-gang-members-brooklyn-schools-recruit-under-
age-girls-hookers-prosecutors-article-1.180295.

136. For more information see www.exoduscry.com.

137. Rebecca Price Janney, *Harriet Tubman* (Bethany House: Minneapolis, 1999), 62.

138. *The Holy Bible, English Standard Version* (Wheaton: Crossway,
2001).

139. Ibid.

140. Allen Verhey and Joseph S. Harvard, *Ephesians* (Louisville:
Westminster John Knox, 2011), 97-98.

141. Francis Foulkes, *The Letter of Paul to the Ephesians: An Introduction and Commentary* (Grand Rapids: Wm. B. Eerdmans
Publishing Company, 1989), 90.

142. John MacArthur, *Ephesians* (Chicago: Moody Publishers,
1986), 70.

143. Ibid., 77.

144. N.T. Wright, "Paul's Gospel and Caesar's Empire," *Center of
Theological Inquiry*, 2002-2004, 3.

145. Mike Bickle, "Studies in the Millennial Kingdom," http://mike-
bickle.org/resources/series/studies-in-the-millennial-kingdom.

146. J. Alec Motyer, *Isaiah* (Downer's Grove: Intervarsity Press,
1993), 491.

147. Richard Cavell, *McLuhan in Space: A Cultural Geography*
(Toronto: University of Toronto Press, 2002), 84-85; "The
Documented Effects of Pornography," accessed March 10,
2012, http://www.forerunner.com/forerunner/X0388_Effects_
of_Pornograp.html; "Unesco Survey Highlights Correlation
Between Media Violence and Youth Perception of Reality,"
accessed March 13, 2012, http://www.unesco.org/bpi/eng/
unescopress/98-32e.htm. Marshall McLuhan wrote in the

1960s regarding the use of media that "we become what we behold". McLuhan, quoting Psalm 113, "They that make them shall become like them", felt that the danger of technology was that it would lead to idolatry and worship of the perceived image of ourselves portrayed by media (narcissim). Another area that this principle is seen in is the use of pornography. It is well documented that viewing pornography increases aggression and violence. Many who view pornography eventually will act out on what they have seen. Others addicted to pornography experience an increase of suicidal thoughts, nightmares, and fear . Evidence has also been documented linking television violence and increase of violence and aggression in children.

148. Philip Edgcumbe Hughes, *A Commentary on the Epistle to the Hebrews* (Grand Rapids: Wm. B. Eerdmans Publishing Company, 1977), 39.

149. Philippians 2:3-11 shows that Jesus' glory and humility are inseparable concepts.

150. A.W. Tozer, *The Knowledge of the Holy* (San Francisco: HarperSanFrancisco, 1961), 13.

151. Gary Craig, *Child Slavery Now: A Contemporary Reader* (Bristol: The Policy Press, 2010), 29.

152. Gethin Chamberlain, "Sold for £20: just two of India's million stolen children", The Guardian, September 6, 2008, accessed April 12, 2012, http://www.guardian.co.uk/world/2008/sep/07/india.humantrafficking; "CHAD: Children sold into slavery for the price of a calf", IRIN Humanitarian News and Analysis, December 21, 2004, accessed April 12, 2012, http://www.irinnews.org/Report/52490/CHAD-Children-sold-into-slavery-for-the-price-of-a-calf; "Percentage of children aged 5-14 engaged in child labour", Childinfo, a division of UNICEF, last updated January 2012, accessed April 12, 2012, http://www.childinfo.org/labour_countrydata.php; "Child Soldiers Trapped in Vicious Cycle of War", UNICEF, February 16, 2005, accessed April 12, 2012, http://www.unicef.org/infobycountry/uganda_25184.html.

153. Joel 3 is one of the key biblical passages about Armageddon.

154. See Stuart Greaves, *Beauty of the Warrior King: The Beauty of Jesus as a Man of War* (2011), mp3.

155. J. Alec Motyer, *Isaiah* (Downer's Grove: Intervarsity Press, 1993), 491.

156. "Children of the World Initiative," *WomenAid International*, accessed April 14, 2012, http://www.womenaid.org/wcwi.htm.

157. "Millennium Development Goals," United Nations Association of the United States of America, accessed April 14, 2012, http://www.unausa.org/page.aspx?pid=866.

158. Elisabeth Rosenthal and Andrew Martin, "UN says solving food crisis could cost $30 Billion," New York Times, June 4, 2008, accessed April 14, 2012, http://www.iht.com/articles/2008/06/04/news/04food.php.

159. Melonie Dodaro, "Review of the movie Fast Food Nation" February 8, 2010, accessed April 14, 2012, http://www.examiner.com/nlp-in-vancouver/review-of-the-movie-fast-food-nation.

160. Petter Stalenheim, Catalina Perdomo, and Elisabeth Skons, SIPRI Yearbook 2008, "Military Expenditure," (Oxford University Press, 2008), accessed April 09, 2012, http://www.sipri.org/yearbook/2008/05.

161. Ronald G. Walters, *American Reformers, 1815-1860* (New York: Hill and Wang, 1997), 80.

162. William Thomas Stead, George Campbell Morgan, *The Welsh Revival* (Boston: The Pilgrim Press, 1905), 44.

163. Wesley L. Duewel, *Revival Fire* (Grand Rapids: Zondervan Publishing House, 1995), 182-183.

164. Fred and Sharon Wright, *World's Greatest Revivals* (Shippensburg: Destiny Image, 2007), 163.

165. Alvin Reid, *Introduction to Evangelism* (Nashville: Broadman & Holman Publishers, 1998), 76.

166. Duewel, 182-183.

167. Stephen Sywulka, "The Selling of A 'Miracle City,'" accessed April 10, 2012, http://www.ctlibrary.com/ct/1999/april5/9t423c.html.

168. Carol Saia, "God Ends Idols 700-year Reign in Almolonga, Guatemala," accessed April 5, 2012, http://www.glowtorch.org/Home/IdolatryendsinAlmolonga/tabid/2767/Default.aspx.

169. *Let the Sea Resound*, DVD. Sentinel Group, 2005; "Fiji in Transformation," accessed April 14, 2012, http://www.fusion-ministry.com/fijivideo.php?page=4.

170. CIA World Factbook, accessed April 11, 2012, https://www.cia.gov/library/publications/the-world-factbook/geos/ha.html.

171. Isaiah is the clearest Old Testament prophet to detail the Father's plan for justice and the activity of the Holy Spirit.

172. *"Blessed are the poor in spirit, for theirs is the kingdom of heaven"* (Matthew 5:3); *"Blessed are you poor, for yours is the kingdom of God"* (Luke 6:20).

173. Separated Parent Access & Resource Center, "Divorce and Fatherhood Statistics," SPARC, accessed April 12, 2012, http://deltabravo.net/custody/stats.php.

174. KSFY, "2011 Youth Risk Behavior Survey results released," accessed April 12, 2012, http://www.ksfy.com/story/17387281/2011-youth-risk-behavior-survey-results-released; "What Is Bullying," accessed April 12, 2012, www.stopbullying.gov; Bullying Statistics, "Bullying and Suicide," accessed April 12, 2012, http://www.bullyingstatistics.org/content/bullying-and-suicide.html.

175. Brother Yun and Paul Hattaway, *The Heavenly Man: The Remarkable True Story of Chinese Christian Brother Yun* (London: Monarch Books, 2004), 255-257.

176. Jim Butschli, "Global pharmaceutical market undergoing dramatic change," accessed April 9, 2012, http://www.ppphar-mapack.com/en/displaynews.html?newsID=100093940.

177. Michael Fleshman, "AIDS Orphans: facing Africa's 'silent crisis,'" accessed April 12, 2012, http://www.un.org/en/

africarenewal/vol15no3/153child.htm; AVERT, AVERTing HIV and AIDS, International HIV and AIDS charity, accessed April 12, 2012, http://www.avert.org/aids-orphans.htm.

178. Lars Brownworth, *Lost to the West: The Forgotten Byzantine Empire that Rescued Western Civilization* (New York: Crown Publishers, 2009), 104-105.

179. Author unknown.

180. Mike Bickle with Brian Kim, *The 7 Commitments of a Forerunner* (Kansas City: Forerunner Publishing, 2009), 11.

About the Author

Stuart Greaves is on the Senior Leadership Team at the International House of Prayer-Kansas City. He gives leadership to the NightWatch, which presently consists of 250 singers, musicians, and intercessors contending for breakthrough. He also directs the African American Forerunner Alliance, a department of IHOP-KC focused on the prophetic role of black believers in the end-time worship movement. Stuart's vision is to reveal Christ by the Holy Spirit to the depths of the hearts of God's people and to proclaim the forerunner message. He also gives leadership to the Haitian Pearl—an organization that focuses on serving Haiti through prayer and works of justice. Stuart travels nationally and internationally teaching on the forerunner message, intercession, and the knowledge of God. He is also part of the leadership and faculty at the International House of Prayer University (IHOPU). Stuart is married to Esther, his wife of 12 years, and currently resides in Kansas City, Missouri.

If you would like to have Stuart speak at your church/ministry, please email:

stuartmgreaves@gmail.com

You can also find him on Facebook at

www.facebook.com/stuartmgreaves

About The International House of Prayer, Kansas City www.ihop.org

What is IHOP-KC?

The International House of Prayer, Kansas City is an international missions organization committed to prayer (intercession, worship, healing, prophesying, etc.); fasting (covering 365 days a year); and the Great Commission (proclaiming Jesus to all nations with power as the way to establish His justice in the earth). The mission of IHOPKC is to call forth, train, and mobilize worshiping intercessors who operate in the forerunner spirit as End Time prophetic messengers; to establish a 24-hour-a-day prayer room in Kansas City as a perpetual solemn assembly that "keeps the sanctuary" by gathering corporately to fast and pray in the spirit of the Tabernacle of David as God's primary method of establishing justice (full revival unto the great harvest); to combine 24/7 prayers for justice with 24/7 works of justice until the Lord returns; to send out teams to plant Houses of Prayer in the nations after God grants a breakthrough of His power in Kansas City. The forerunner spirit operates in God's grace in context to the fasted lifestyle (Matt. 6) and prepares others to live in wholehearted love by proclaiming the beauty of Jesus as Bridegroom, King, and Judge. Our work includes equipping and sending missionaries as dedicated intercessors and anointed messengers working to see revival in the church and a great harvest among the lost.

Find out more about the following on our website www.ihop.org:

* International House of Prayer University

* Internships & Training Programs

* Children's Equipping Center

* Hope City: an inner city prayer room in downtown Kansas City that includes evangelism, restoring lives and making disciples; a compassion ministry, church on the streets, and soup kitchen. Visit our website for more on Hope City Intensive training program www.ihop.org/hopecity/

* Forerunner Music: represents worship leaders at IHOP-KC

* Events and Conferences, including our Onething annual conference held in December in Kansas City, Missouri

Whether you are interested in visiting IHOP-KC, receiving the Missions Base podcast, browsing the bookstore, watching live Webcasts, or enrolling in IHOPU's eschool courses, the website delivers the information you need and offers many opportunities to feed your heart with resources. With login capabilities that expose you to even more comprehensive IHOP-KC materials, we hope our site will become an ongoing resource for many years to come. Some of the website features include:

* Podcasting

* MP3 Downloads

* Forums

* Free Webstream of our 24-7 Prayer Room: live worship and intercession on the internet, any hour, any day, any place, in your home, in your office, in your dorm, on your mobile device.) Join us @ www.ihop.org/prayerroom

* Sermon and Teaching Notes

* eSchool Distance Learning through IHOPU

* Internship Applications

· Prayer Room Blogs

· Online Bookstore

International House of Prayer University

Redefining theological education through night and day prayer, IHOPU combines biblical training with practical discipleship and ministry experience for students who want to encounter God in His Word in an environment of 24/7 worship-based prayer. Our schools train men and women for a life of devotion and service to God, preparing them for partnership with Him in His plan to bring transformation to every sphere of society. We invite you to learn about our schools of ministry, worship, and media at www.ihop.org/ihopu/ or by contacting us by phone (816-763-0243) or mail (12444 Grandview Rd, Grandview, MO 64030).

* Forerunner School of Ministry Programs:

  • Justice Ministry

  • House of Prayer Leadership

  • Biblical and Theological Studies

  • Healing and Prophecy

  • Children and Youth Ministry

* Forerunner Music Academy Programs

  • Music Production

  • Prophetic Worship

* Forerunner Media Institute: includes training in live production, core technical classes, and core messenger classes.

* IHOPU eSchool Distance Learning: brings class content of IHOPU directly to you through online

courses through downloadable lectures, course notes, and discussion forums that give you the full experience of being a student at IHOPU. Available for credit or non-credit, or group study courses. www.ihop.org/eschool

IHOP-KC Internships

IHOP-KC offers a variety of three-month and six-month internships for all ages. All internships have the same basic components including prayer meetings, classroom instruction, practical ministry experience, community fellowship and team building, conference participation, practical service, and Bible study. Attendees regularly participate in prayer meetings—between fifteen and twenty-five hours a week—in the prayer room, which can include worship team involvement, intercession for revival, personal devotional time, and study of the Word. Education and instruction cover a wide range of topics including: Christian foundations, prayer, worship, intimacy with God, the Bridal Paradigm of the Kingdom of God, the prophetic and healing ministries, serving the poor, and many others. The IHOP-KC website www.ihop.org has information on all of our internships, including:

* Fire in the Night is a nighttime internship for those ages eighteen to thirty that want to worship and minister to the Lord through the night, midnight to 6:00 a.m. It consists of two, three-month tracks. Participants may choose to do one or both tracks. This program includes housing and eighteen meals a week.

* Onething is a six-month daytime internship for young adults ages eighteen to twenty-five who are singers, musicians, intercessors, or evangelists. This program includes housing and eighteen meals a week.

* Intro to IHOP-KC is a three-month internship for people of all ages, married or single, who want to learn and experience all that IHOP-KC represents—prayer, worship, intimacy, etc.

* Simeon Company is a three-month training program for people ages fifty and older who refuse to retire in their desire to radically serve Jesus through prayer, fasting, and worship.

* Awakening Teen Camps and Intensives consist of one to six week programs and conferences focused on teaching teens about their identity in God, intimacy with Jesus, and intercession, so that they would have a lasting impact for the kingdom of God. Includes Teen Fascinate Conference.

Forerunner Music www.forerunnermusic.com

Forerunner Music represents worship leaders at the International House of Prayer in Kansas City (IHOP-KC), a 24/7 ministry of prayer and worship before the Lord that never stops. While live worship has continually burned at IHOP-KC, the prayer room has become a spiritual greenhouse for musical creativity. Forerunner Music was birthed out of our desire to share the melodies created here with the Body of Christ. The artists represented are worship leaders and songwriters at IHOP-KC who express the message of abandonment to Jesus and love for Him through song, as King David did.

Simple Devotion (CD)

Worship from the IHOP-KC NightWatch is a twelve-song, eleven-artist collection of songs from this dedicated group of worshipers who minister to the Lord during the night hours. *Simple*

Devotion, mellow and inspiring, represents the hearts of our nightly worship and intercession.

Constant (CD)

A compilation album that is steady and lyrically inspiring with songs thematic of the faithfulness of God, His greatness, and our great need for Him.

Featuring music of eleven different IHOP-KC worship leaders and songwriters, it showcases the rich musical diversity found on the Missions Base. Artists Include: Misty Edwards, Luke Wood, Jordan Johnson, Jon Thurlow, Tim Cone, Alisha Powell, Brandon Hampton, Seth Parks, Audra Lynn, Sarah Edwards, and Jenny Powell.

Joy (CD)

Live worship highlights from the IHOPU student awakening. Many of the songs on this album were birthed as a result of a move of the Holy Spirit that began in our midst on November 11, 2009.

Fling Wide (CD)

Experience a live evening of worship recorded during an IHOP-KC service. This seamless flow of worship led by Misty Edwards and her team is a raw, live album with songs including, "Fling Wide," "Rend," and "Arms Wide Open." These songs, birthed in the prayer room, convey abandonment to Jesus, loyalty to His truth, and a desire to impact the world with the love and power of God.

IN THE RIGHT HANDS, THIS BOOK WILL CHANGE LIVES!

Most of the people who need this message will not be looking for this book. To change their lives, you need to put a copy of this book in their hands.

> But others (seeds) fell into good ground, and brought forth fruit, some a hundred-fold, some sixty-fold, some thirty-fold (Matthew 13:8).

Our ministry is constantly seeking methods to find the good ground, the people who need this anointed message to change their lives. Will you help us reach these people?

> Remember this—a farmer who plants only a few seeds will get a small crop. But the one who plants generously will get a generous crop (2 Corinthians 9:6).

EXTEND THIS MINISTRY BY SOWING
3 BOOKS, 5 BOOKS, 10 BOOKS, **OR MORE TODAY,**
AND BECOME A LIFE CHANGER!

Thank you,

Don Nori Sr., Founder
Destiny Image
Since 1982